Challenging

Kathleen Jones is Emeritus Professor of Social Policy in the University of York and an Hon. Fellow of the Royal College of Psychiatrists. She is the author of eleven books and many reports and journal articles on policy issues in the health and social services, two books on religious poetry and six on the lives of the Christian saints. She is an Anglican and a former member of the General Synod of the Church of England.

Challenging
Richard Dawkins

Kathleen Jones

CANTERBURY
PRESS
Norwich

First published in 2007 by the Canterbury Press Norwich
(a publishing imprint of Hymns Ancient & Modern
Limited, a registered charity)
13–17 Long Lane, London EC1A 9PN

www.scm-canterburypress.co.uk

British Library Cataloguing in Publication data

A catalogue record for this book is available
from the British Library

ISBN 978-1-85311 841 8

Typeset by Regent Typesetting, London
Printed and bound by CPI Bookmarque, Croydon, CR0 4TD

Contents

Preface

In *The God Delusion*, published in the autumn of 2006, Professor Richard Dawkins tells his readers that God is not dead, as Nietzsche told us: God never existed in the first place.

Religion – any kind of religion – is, he maintains, a massive delusion: 'A persistent false belief held in the face of strong contradictory evidence' (p. 5). Jews, Muslims, Hindus, Sikhs, Buddhists and others are as deluded as Christians, their beliefs founded on lies and hypocrisy. He urges his readers to imagine a world without religion, as John Lennon did: there would be no wars, he says, no terrorism, no massacres, no beheadings, no floggings and mutilations. Serbs and Croats, Israelis and Arabs would all live peaceably with one another. The Crusades would never have happened. The Gunpowder Plot would never have happened. India would not be split from Pakistan. The Twin Towers would never have been reduced to Ground Zero, and there would have been no bombings on the London Underground. No 9/11, no 7/7.

What a promise. What an appeal it has today in a frightened and uncertain world.

People with a religious faith will think that Richard Dawkins is deeply and tragically wrong, but it has to be said that he sounds in most respects disarmingly mild. As he says, he does not go about beheading people, or otherwise inflicting physical harm on them. Words are his only weapon. He writes with real affection about his wife, Lalla Ward, a television actress and scriptwriter, who reads his drafts aloud to him. He wrote a very touching letter to his daughter Juliet when she was ten (more of that later). He rides, or used to ride, a bicycle. When he gets cross about things, he goes and digs in the garden. He likes people of any nationality, as long as they are not professing religion. He likes women, he likes children. He hates violence, he hates prejudice, but he hates religion more.

Professor Dawkins is a zoologist. Unlike his hero Charles Darwin (who spent much time in his boyhood collecting beetles by the hundred, and staking them out in rows for inspection) he works with live animals rather than dead ones. He tells us many interesting things, like why giraffes have long necks, and why bats fly by night. He also tell us that the chimpanzee and the human share about 99.5 per cent of their history; that evolution and natural selection are the only principles that order the universe; that the universal law of nature is that the strong and powerful survive, and the weak die off.

He has been pursuing these ideas in print for more than three decades. His first major book, *The Selfish Gene*, was published in 1976. This is based on the premise that 'we are survival machines blindly programmed to preserve the selfish molecules called genes'. Genes, we are told, are like Chicago gangsters. 'The predominant quality to be expected of a successful gene is ruthless selfishness.'

Since then, he has written a series of other books on the same theme, and he has not changed his mind about the ruthlessness of genes; but his latest book, *The God Delusion*, shows a change of focus. He still insists that the survival of the fittest is the only basic principle of human and animal existence, but he has moved to an all-out attack on religion. Religious belief, he tells us, is the main cause of war, a weapon for intolerance and terrorism. Atheism stands for altruism and peaceful co-existence. He argues that Science is based on reason, while Religion is simply based on superstition. People must be rescued from the hypocrisy of belief. At the end of the book he appends a 'partial list of addresses, for individuals needing support in escaping from religion', including a website emanating from Colorado Springs called 'Internet Infidels'. In the same year as the book's publication, he established a foundation to provide British schools with anti-religious literature, and computer material to teach the children that religion of any kind is harmful. It is called the Richard Dawkins Foundation for Reason and Science, or RDFRS for short.

Richard Dawkins has spent many thousands of words decrying what he calls 'The God Hypothesis': the idea that God exists, that there is meaning and purpose in human life; and he has brought back into circulation some very dated nineteenth-century arguments about the conflict between 'Science' and 'Religion'. *Déjà vu* all over again, as Woody Allen put it.

Do we really need to go over all that again in the twenty-first century? It seems that we do. The rise of religious fundamentalism has led to new forms of intolerance in both East and West, and led many peaceable tolerant people to be chary of expressing religious views of any kind. Some people may be taking Richard Dawkins' word for it that atheism is a better recipe for social harmony than faith. The old chorus that there is 'no evidence' for the existence of God, the old cries of 'Prove it!' again trickle through the correspondence columns of the press. The charge that religion is responsible for all the evils of the world is not a new one, but it needs to be answered afresh in our fractured and fearful society.

I hope that other writers will be moved to answer it in their own terms. Some have already done so. Professor Alister McGrath, a former atheist and scientist, now an Oxford professor of theology, has written a theological reply in *Dawkins' God: Genes, Memes and the Meaning of Life* (2004) and *The Dawkins Delusion* (2007), and he quotes some other early skirmishes in what looks like becoming a protracted battle. For my own part, I write as a Christian, a member of the Anglican Communion, and a social scientist with a background in history and social philosophy. My research area is the dynamics and management of closed institutions: special hospitals, closed psychiatric units, prisons, concentration camps: the study of human beings in captivity, not of animals in the wild.

Richard Dawkins says that he hates dogma, and he says it in the most dogmatic terms. Academics usually use more gentlemanly (or ladylike) weapons than the bludgeon. They write things like 'Professor A is mistaken in his assumption that . . .', or 'Dr B may have overlooked C's definitive analysis of . . .'; but his critique is so crude that it needs to be challenged bluntly, and without equivocation.

Much as he will dislike the thought, his attack, if analysed and assessed, can make a useful basis for meeting the claims that there is 'no evidence' for the existence of God and the practice of faith; and believers – Christians, Jews, Muslims, Hindus and members of other faiths – may benefit from his challenges by clarifying their own beliefs. He has some uncomfortably sharp things to say about our comfortable assumptions; and we need to know what we believe and why we believe it.

This study has been written against the backdrop of war and rumours of war, of explosions in Baghdad and Tel Aviv and Kabul, of television images of exhausted soldiers, bewildered women and frightened, crying children. Cheap and easy air travel, information technology and mass migration have forced together ideas and beliefs which have been separated in previous centuries by distance and slow communication. No sooner has a disaster occurred than a thousand images flood the television screens of the world, and we start counting the coffins. The whole world is like a gear box that has lost its lubrication. The gears grind when we try to move; and it hurts. We shriek 'Stop it!', and yet the chaos and the killing go on.

We live in a compensation culture, and people cast around looking for someone to blame. It is very easy for them to blame 'religion', to end up sitting on the fence, puzzled and disturbed, saying, 'All these different religions – they can't all be right, can they?' What's real and what isn't? How do we judge? How do we know? How can anyone believe in a good God? What about the terrible state of the world?

Why are the issues so complicated? Because the modern world is complicated, and Richard Dawkins' writing is complicated. He assumes that his readers understand a good deal of biology, but that they will accept his sweeping (and often unfounded) assertions about all other subjects, including cosmology, particle physics and quantum mechanics, theology, history and the social sciences. Examining his arguments requires a broad perspective and a variety of frames of reference. He presents his readers with a body of information and disinformation which has to be disentangled and analysed with some care.

There are no quick and easy answers; but the exercise is worth undertaking. If God is not real, merely a projection of our own wishes, desires and prejudices, Richard Dawkins is clearly right: the human race has wasted an immense amount of time and effort over the centuries on what is no more than a mass delusion. If he is wrong (and I think he is) then God is the reality on which everything else in human life depends. And it matters.

Acknowledgements

I would like to thank students and academic colleagues of many different backgrounds, nationalities and religious affiliations who have been willing to discuss Richard Dawkins' writing over the years, and have offered many valuable insights and criticisms. I am especially grateful to Alice Clay, who said it was 'more fun than following the Da Vinci Code', and two other good friends who might prefer not to be named: a professor of physics who checked the scientific data in Chapter 2, and conceded that 'there might be something in this God business', and a nun who has trustingly prayed for my endeavours although she knows that I am not of her fold.

I have never met Professor Richard Dawkins – and that is probably just as well, because we would have much to disagree about. I am concerned here only with his public pronouncements and their effect on more impressionable minds than mine; but I would at least like to thank him for stirring up some very lively discussions.

I

The World of Richard Dawkins

Richard Dawkins believes that human beings are unimportant – merely incidental to the process of biological evolution. In *The Selfish Gene*, published over 30 years ago, he wrote, 'Individuals are not stable things – they are fleeting . . . Genes, like diamonds, are forever.'[1] He argues that the gene is the unit of evolution, because it struggles for survival from generation to generation. Individuals and animals have no lasting significance, and there is no purpose in human existence. This bleak philosophy proved very popular with the reading public. By the time he wrote *The God Delusion* in 2006, he had produced six other books on different aspects of the same theme: *The Extended Phenotype* (1982), *The Blind Watchmaker* (1986), *River Out of Eden* (1995), *Climbing Mount Improbable* (1996), *Unweaving the Rainbow* (1998) and *A Devil's Chaplain: Selected Essays* (2003). The eight volumes show a remarkable consistency of purpose as he develops his views on evolutionary theory, and increasingly moves to an uncompromising atheism in which religion is caricatured and ridiculed.

How does he see the world? In *Unweaving the Rainbow* (1998), he recommends an exercise to illustrate his view of the evolutionary process.[2] He suggests that readers try it: 'Fling your arms wide in an expansive gesture to span all of evolution from its origin at your left fingertip to today at your right fingertip.' Is he saying that human life is represented by this broad span? No, he is not. He is saying that it represents *all* life, beginning with bacteria. In fact, most of the span is taken up with bacteria: 'All the way across your midline to well past your right shoulder, life consists of nothing but bacteria.' Human beings do not start for a long time yet: 'Many-celled, invertebrate life flowers somewhere about your right elbow. The dinosaurs originate about the middle of your right palm, and go extinct around your last finger joint.' There is still no sign of the human race when the dinosaurs die off (destroyed, he says, by showers of meteorites). 'The whole story of *Homo sapiens* and our predecessor *Homo erectus* is contained in the thickness of one nail-clipping.' All of us, ever since we came down from the trees about 45,000 years ago, he tells us.

In the long, slow evolution of life on earth, human beings are latecomers. If the whole story of *Homo sapiens* and *Homo erectus* is contained in that nail-clipping, what price history? He says that the Sumerians, the Babylonians, the Jewish patri-archs, the dynasties of the Pharaohs, the legions of Rome, the Christian Fathers, Napoleon and Hitler, the Beatles and Bill Clinton are all 'blown away in the dust from one light stroke of the nail file'.

In this illustration, Richard Dawkins has very astutely chosen his own grounds for debate. He starts on our own small planet, with the emergence of the earliest life forms – but that is surely too late. If we are to consider whether we have a Creator, we have to go back to the creation of the universe, not to start on earth with the bacteria. He tells us that human history is brief and meaningless in his perspective; but he has very neatly managed to ignore the rest of the cosmos by con-centrating on our own planet. He has said nothing about the solar system, the galaxy and the many galaxies beyond it. In fact, he has not even covered the whole history of the world: only its history since life began, and that is mostly the history of bacteria. He has chosen his own grounds for debate. Then he has measured living creatures only in terms of time, and not of quality. One stroke of the nail file, and we all disappear.

This is a biologist's professional frame of reference, and it is a very limited one. Richard Dawkins maintains that we need 'a good dose of science, the honest and systematic endeavour to find out the truth about the real world', but the science behind his illustration takes no account of knowledge in any scientific field except his own. He argues that the model of the world on which human beings operate is the model our ancestors needed in order to survive in it. 'The simulation software was constructed and designed by natural selection, and it is most adept in the world of our ancestors on the African savannah.'[3] This is a very compressed and somewhat obscure statement. The reference to 'simulation software' seems to mean that he regards human beings as inefficient computers. In *Who's Who*, he gives his only hobby as 'the Apple Mac'. The African savannah is brought into the argument because he returns repeatedly to the idea that we are not very far down the evolutionary line from the chimpanzee. This fits in very well with his own childhood experience: he tells us quite a lot about his boyhood on his website[4] and in his books, and how early influences shaped his thinking.

The making of an evolutionist

Richard Dawkins was born in Uganda, and moved to Kenya with his parents at the age of two. East Africa evidently had a profound influence on him. In *The God Delusion*, he writes of looking at the stars, 'heady with the night scents of frangipanni and trumpet flowers in an African garden'.[5] In *A Devil's Chaplain*, he writes: 'Africa was my personal cradle . . . I am one of those (it includes most people who have ever spent time south of the Sahara) who think of Africa as a place of enchantment.'[6] He went back once, in 1994, to look for his old home, but failed to find it. He was only there for a week, and he spent it on safari. He does not seem to have been interested in the problems of modern East Africa – the devastation of AIDS, the political corruption, the desperate poverty and the hungry children; but he was there as a child in the late colonial period, the 1940s. He is not really thinking in terms of modern Africa. He is only interested in the mythical Africa of the first hominids: a biologist's alternative to the Garden of Eden.

He went to an English public school, Oundle. One might expect that he reacted against public school religion, but this was not the case. He says: 'I didn't have religion forced down my throat',[7] and he attended chapel without complaint. He liked the school chaplain, whom he describes as 'a decent liberal clergyman', and imagines him looking up at the night sky and having a deeply religious experience; but Richard Dawkins' reaction to the night sky was different. The early African experience stayed with him. He remembered the stars blazing in the darkness of an African night, and the animals he had seen on the savannah roaming and killing.[8] In another of his books, he comments that 'the racing elegance of cheetahs and gazelles is bought at huge cost in blood, and the suffering of countless antecedents on both sides'.[9] Like Charles Darwin, he reacted against 'the clumsy, wasteful, blundering, low and horridly cruel works of nature'. One can see that the African experience was the source of his fascination with the animal world, and the source of his distress at what creatures did to each other.

Biology lessons must have fallen on receptive ears. He learned that human beings were descended from chimpanzees, and that the whole human race originated from his beloved East Africa. He rejected religion, and became enthusiastic about Darwin's *On the Origin of Species*. He went on to take

4

a degree in biology at Oxford, and followed it by five years' doctoral work in zoology under the supervision of an eminent ethologist. Ethology is the branch of zoology that is concerned with animal behaviour – live animals, not dead ones. The public image of a biologist is of someone who dissects animals, but Richard Dawkins clearly identifies with them as fellow-creatures. After taking his doctorate, he went to the United States, and became an Assistant Professor in Zoology at Berkeley, University of California. He returned to Oxford in 1970 as a Lecturer in Zoology. He became a Reader in Zoology in 1989, three years after writing *The Selfish Gene*, which was an immediate success.

There seem to be two reasons for its popularity. One is that the general public had become very interested in apes as a result of the writing and television presentations of Desmond Morris, who was the curator of the London Zoo. He wrote *The Naked Ape* (1967), followed by *The Human Zoo* (1969). The proposition that the human race might be descended from monkeys was hardly news more than a century after Darwin, but Morris brought the parallels to life, and became a celebrity. When he took an early retirement to Cyprus, there was a space waiting for a literary zoologist. The second reason was that *The Selfish Gene* was timely in political terms. In 1976, Margaret Thatcher had recently become leader of the Conservative Party, Britain was nearly bankrupt, and the welfare state was very much under attack.[10] People were ready to be told that survival is the name of the game, self-interest is good, and the weak inevitably go to the wall. Richard Dawkins was pressing all the right buttons.

In *The Selfish Gene*, he talks repeatedly of genes 'co-operating' with each other, but genes do not have human will and make moral choices. If they do 'co-operate', it is after the fashion of the Mafia or the Ku Klux Klan, and they are not appropriate models for human behaviour. He admits that human beings are not entirely conditioned by their self-ish genes – he does say 'Genes aren't us' – but he pushes the concept of natural selection far beyond Darwin's limits.[11] Other well-known ethologists, such as Konrad Lorenz,[12] draw a distinction between human beings and their animal ancestors on the grounds that human beings have a much more advanced capacity for learning, and that nurturing is therefore much more important than it is in the animal world. The Oxford University website calls Richard Dawkins 'the first true ethologist of the gene', but that is extending the scope of ethology well beyond the limits that most ethologists would recognize.

Political values have changed since *The Selfish Gene* was first published. Richard Dawkins had an opportunity to revise the text when he published the thirtieth-anniversary edition, but he published it unaltered. He did write a new preface, in which he complained that people had put the emphasis on *selfish*, when he meant them to put it on *gene*; and he pointed out that he had said in the first edition, 'Let us try to *teach* altruism, for we are born selfish.' He said that he might have entitled the book *The Altruistic Vehicle* or *The Co-operative Gene*, but this claim does not really carry conviction. Those titles would not have been popular in the Britain of the late 1970s.

The success of the book may have taken him by surprise. There is no indication in his writing that he thinks much about politics. Three years after its publication, he became Reader in Zoology at Oxford, and in 1995, he became the first and so far the only Charles Simonyi Professor of the Public Understanding of Science in the University of Oxford. This is a personal Chair, privately endowed, not a regular university appointment. The title suggests that Richard Dawkins is an expert on all aspects of scientific development and how they can be communicated to the general public; but zoology is not one of the disciplines that are at the cutting edge of science today. He has little interest in recent scientific discoveries in cosmology or particle physics, and he is mystified by quantum mechanics, which has the potential to span both fields. He writes extensively about genes, but he is not a geneticist in the sense that the scientists who work on DNA are geneticists. His professorial title is a very broad one, but his area of expertise is comparatively narrow.

It is interesting to learn how Richard Dawkins came to be appointed to his prestigious and impressive-sounding post. He makes it clear that he did not know Charles Simonyi at the time of his appointment, though they are good friends now.[13] It seems that their interests and enthusiasms are very similar. Charles Simonyi is a multi-millionaire, born in Budapest, with a record as a brilliant computer engineer. He emigrated to the United States, joined Xerox, and then applied personally to Bill Gates, and moved to Microsoft. He was leader of the team that developed WORD.[14] He is a qualified pilot with many hours' flying time, and is passionate about space travel. His website is called 'Charlesinspace.com', and in April 2007, he spent ten days at the NASA space station. That trip is said to have cost him £25 million, so endowing the Oxford Chair in the Public Understanding of Science in perpetuity must have been well within his means. Apparently he drew up detailed specifications for the post, and the sort of person he wanted to be appointed to it. It seems likely that he wanted someone who shared his fascination with computers; someone with a sound academic record, and ideas to promote; someone with an established literary reputation, whose books sold well. We are not told whether he specified an evolutionist or an atheist, but it seems probable that Richard Dawkins' literary work has his benefactor's approval.

'Coming out' as an atheist

As Richard Dawkins continued to publish his views, he increasingly claimed to speak for the whole of the scientific community, and to move steadily from ethology to an attack on religion. 'To be an atheist', he writes in *The God Delusion*, 'is a realistic ambition, and a brave and splendid one. You can be an atheist who is happy, balanced, morally and intellectually fulfilled.' An atheist can face ultimate annihilation unafraid, and take pride in his unbelief, 'standing tall to face the far horizon'.[15] Atheists must 'come out' – like gays. He admits that religious belief is found in all periods of human history, and all cultures – but he claims that it is time to say openly that it is no more than mass delusion.

He maintains that he is 'a deeply religious non-believer'. By this, he apparently means that he thinks deeply about religious issues, and has considered his position carefully. He spends some pages in the early chapters of *The God Delusion* explaining that he is not a theist (someone who believes in God, as members of the major world religions do), nor a deist (someone who believes in some sort of God, not very clearly defined), nor an agnostic (somebody who cannot decide whether God exists or not, and reserves judgement on the matter). He is a 100 per cent campaigning atheist.

Being an atheist is nothing to be apologetic about. It is something to be proud of, standing tall to face the far horizon, for atheism always indicates a healthy independence of mind, and indeed a healthy mind. There are many people who know in their heart of hearts that they are atheists, but dare not admit it to their families, or even, in some cases, to themselves.[16]

The implication is that many more people would declare themselves atheists if they had the courage to resist peer-group pressure, and realized how many people agreed with them:

> The reason that most people don't notice atheists is that many of us are reluctant to 'come out'. My dream is that this book may help people to come out. Exactly as in the case of the gay movement, the more people come out, the easier it will be for others to join them.[17]

He hopes to reach a situation in which a 'critical mass' of atheists can be achieved. There seems to be no doubt that he is in earnest about this endeavour. What he tells his readers of his personal history helps to explain why he is not a believer, but it does not explain the unusual force of his attack.

Darwin and natural selection

In calling himself a Darwinist, Richard Dawkins evokes the scientific uproar that followed the publication of Charles Darwin's *On the Origin of Species*, and the ensuing controversy concerning the religious and the scientific explanations of the origin of life; but he glosses over several important issues: Charles Darwin was the first to propound the theory of natural selection, but not the first to study what he was careful to call 'the theory of evolution'. The link between human beings and apes has never been scientifically demonstrated. Dawkins' exposition takes him far beyond Darwin's more modest conclusions.

There was a good deal of discussion on the subject in the early nineteenth century. Charles Darwin's grandfather, Erasmus Darwin, was one of the leading contributors to the debate – though he studied plants, not animals. Charles Darwin's major contribution was the concept of natural selection, outlined in *On The Origin of Species* (1856), which drew on his field studies in the Galapagos Islands 20 years earlier. Richard Dawkins explains natural selection very clearly. It means the survival of the fittest, but that is not the same as random survival. Take 'the useful device known as the sieve'. You have a hole and a collection of random objects above it. You put the random objects in the sieve. Some force shakes and jostles it. The objects smaller than the hole fall through the sieve, and the larger ones do not.[18] The result is not random, it is selective. In *The Blind Watchmaker*, he argues that giraffes do not have long necks because they adapted to circumstances and needed to reach the tender leaves on the tops of the tallest trees. Acquired characteristics cannot be transmitted. Giraffes have long necks because only the ones with the long necks survived to transmit their genes to the next generation.[19]

In Darwinian terms, if we ask what sort of human beings are 'the fittest' who survive and do not fall through the holes in the sieve, the answer is clear: not those with the highest moral standards. Not the most useful members of society. Not the most intelligent. The survivors will be the toughest, the most ruthless, the most determined to survive.

Darwin seems to have been alarmed at the conclusions to which his field studies led him. He was afraid that people would call him 'a devil's chaplain', and Richard Dawkins took the phrase from him for a book title. Darwin kept his material unpublished for over 20 years because he thought that Victorian society would be outraged by his findings. It was only when another naturalist, Alfred Russel Wallace, sent him his own work, based on field work in the Malay Archipelago and leading to similar conclusions, that he finally agreed to go public. The issues were debated at the British Association Conference in Oxford in 1860.

Darwin had been careful to apply the theory of evolution

only to animals, but members of the audience were quick to apply his ideas to the human race. Professor T. H. Huxley spoke for Darwin. Samuel Wilberforce, Bishop of Oxford and chaplain to the Prince Consort, asked Huxley whether he claimed descent from an ape on his grandfather's side or his grandmother's side – a sneer which showed he had not understood the whole discussion. What Huxley said, in rounded Victorian prose, according to an eye-witness, was:

> I should feel it no shame to have risen from such an origin. But I should feel it a shame to have sprung from one who prostituted the gifts of culture and of eloquence to the service of prejudice and falsehood.[20]

It was a magisterial reproof.

The scientific community was readily convinced that Darwin was right, and the stage was set for the grand battle between science and religion which Richard Dawkins seems to be trying to replay in the twenty-first century. Wilberforce was known to the irreverent as 'Soapy Sam', and something of a theological backwoodsman. Gradually, most thinking people were convinced by Darwin's obvious honesty and his weight of scholarly evidence. *On The Origin of Species* became a bestseller. The development of the steamship meant a great boost to exploration, and before long, natural history museums like the splendid one in London's South Kensington were providing ample evidence that Darwin was right. Most thinking churchmen took the view that Christian belief was not conditional on the assumption that the world was made in six days of earthly time. By 1884, the theologian Frederick Temple delivered the Bampton Lectures, and assumed that the theory of evolution was generally accepted. There were no protests, and 12 years later Temple became Archbishop of Canterbury. By the time Darwin published *The Descent of*

Man in 1876, in which he related human beings to the African primates, his ideas were widely accepted. It seemed that the battle was over.

Darwin might have found Richard Dawkins' views surprising, and more than a little dogmatic. The scientist who made the early contributions to gene theory was not Darwin but his contemporary, Father Gregor Mendel.[21] He was a botanist, and his main work was a study of factorial inheritance on successive generations of peas. Richard Dawkins hardly mentions him, except to complain that he never got in touch with Darwin.[22] Mendel was a German-speaking Augustinian canon in a religious community in Austria, which meant that his scientific contacts were rather limited. His vocation may account for Richard Dawkins' attitude to his work. Mendel was a member of his religious order first, and a botanist second. He gave up his botanical studies to become abbot of his monastery in Silesia. Though he made reports on his findings in Austria, and published them in German, it was a long time before British scientists were alerted to his findings. They are now regarded as the foundation of subsequent work on DNA, but Richard Dawkins continues to promote Darwin and to ignore Mendel. In a paper entitled 'Darwin Triumphant', he says that 'Darwin's achievement, like Einstein's was universal and timeless',[23] and Mendel is not even mentioned.

Anthropologists and archaeologists have long sought for the 'missing link' between the apes (chimpanzees are the closest to human beings in biological terms) and human beings. Richard Dawkins is convinced that the link exists, but is apparently resigned to the fact that the skeletons of the ape-people will probably never be discovered.[24] In most of his writing, he assumes that genetic mutation occurs very slowly over long periods of time, and if this were the case, we might expect that the bones of the 'missing link' would have been unearthed in many places by now; but he contradicts his own argument about gradualism by proposing 'a leap in genetic space'. That suggests that human beings and apes are not that close after all. Human beings and chimpanzees cannot mate, but he indulges in some gleeful speculations on what would happen if they could:

> The news would be earth-shattering. Bishops would bleat, lawyers would gloat in anticipation, conservative politicians would thunder, socialists wouldn't know where to put their barricades. The scientist that achieved the feat would be drummed out of the senior common room, denounced in pulpit and gutter press, condemned, perhaps by an Ayatollah's *fatwah*.[25]

The 'African Eve'

Richard Dawkins' training as a biologist leads him to formulate the evolution of the human race in matriarchal terms rather than the patriarchal terms still used by many followers of the major world religions. Devout Jews, Christians and Muslims sometimes have difficulty in realizing that the early Jewish Scriptures, which are common to all three, have come down to us from a pastoral and patriarchal society in which to call God 'Father' was the highest praise his followers could offer him. Though many now think of the Creator – maker of both male and female – as beyond gender, the old phraseology and the assumptions that accompany it linger on.

Biologists take a very different view. Speculation that the first ape that came down from the tree and stood upright was female is widely accepted, and has been eagerly seized upon by some feminists. This fragment of pre-historical speculation is so much at odds with the traditions of both the Eastern and Western worlds about gender roles that it requires some explanation.

It is a very different story from the biblical accounts of the creation of the first man and the first woman. In *River Out of Eden*, Richard Dawkins explains the biology of inheritance in some detail.[26] Human beings, and many other forms of life, are dependent on mitochondria – tiny bodies inside every cell in their bodies – for breaking down food and turning it into energy. Without mitochondria, we would die very quickly; but they are only transmitted from mother to daughter down the generations. A son will inherit mitochondria from his mother, but cannot in turn transmit them to his children. This is because, although there are a few in the sperm, they are located in its tail, and that breaks off at the time of conception. The egg, on the other hand, is much larger, and has millions of mitochondria in readiness. So a baby gets its mitochondria from its mother, and she derives her mitochondria from her mother, and so on back through history – a great chain of mothers and daughters bearing life. Geneticists have developed the 'African Eve' hypothesis: that all human beings can be traced back to one great female ancestor from whom we inherit our mitochondria. So the first *Homo sapiens* was actually female.[27] When he wrote the first draft of *The Blind Watchmaker*, Richard Dawkins was so attached to the African Eve that he referred to God as 'she' all through; but when he showed the manuscript to a feminist, she told him he was being patronizing. So he is forced to refer to the God he does not believe in as 'he', but this is only for lack of a gender-free pronoun.

'Meme theory'

All Richard Dawkins' explanations are biological explanations. He pays very little attention to other branches of science, and none at all to any other subject of study. He has a very ingenious explanation for ignoring history, geography, philosophy, theology and other subjects which might broaden his perspective. He calls them 'memes'. He first introduced the concept of 'meme theory' in *The Selfish Gene*, and developed it in subsequent books. There is no such word as 'meme' in the dictionaries. He invented it himself, 'to convey the idea of a unit of cultural transmission or a unit of imitation'.[28]

The examples he gives of memes include tunes, catchphrases, ideas, clothes, fashions, ways of making pots or of building arches. His examples of 'meme activity' include 'stitches in knitting, knots in ropes or fishing nets, origami folding patterns, useful tricks in carpentry or pottery, or making a model Chinese junk'. It is not clear in what respects these activities are thought to be 'like' gene transmission, or 'like' the development of religion. He argues that survival of 'the god meme' (religion) is a result of its psychological appeal: 'It provides a superficially plausible answer to deep and troubling questions about our own existence.' He compares it to a doctor's placebo, 'which is none the less effective for being imaginary'.[29] He can see no connection between 'the god meme' and the selfish behaviour of genes (which Christians call original sin) or with the effort required to be altruistic (which they call love or compassion).

He writes: 'Just as genes propagate themselves in the gene pool by leaping from body to body via sperm or eggs, so memes propagate themselves in the meme pool by leaping from brain to brain.' All that he seems to mean by this is that people communicate ideas. He complains in *The Selfish Gene* that philosophy and 'the subjects known as humanities' are still 'being taught as though Darwin never lived'.[30]

He reduces ideas, including religious ideas, to the level of knitting or pot-making. Or a new hat. Every time he says 'just as . . .', or tells the reader that two things are alike, one should look out for a very slippery slope. If he were a specialist in English grammar, he would know the differences between a simile, a metaphor, an analogy and an allegory. All involve some resemblance between the items compared. Religious ideas are not at all like making pots or Chinese junks. There is no resemblance, the use of a descriptive form is not remotely applicable, the cases are not parallel, and there is no figurative or symbolical meaning. His 'just as . . .' is usually the mark of a verbal trick.

In *A Devil's Chaplain,* he says that he derived the word from the Greek *mimeme,* meaning 'similar', and notes its similarity to the French *même.* He has a section on 'The Infected Mind' in which he describes religions as 'mind parasites', and makes an analogy with computer viruses: 'the viral analogy is always in my mind when I consider religion'. He boasts that his invented word has 'half a million hits on the Web' and insists that memes 'have at least a superficial analogy to genetic transmission'.[31]

Then he says that that religious messages are 'easily subverted by nuns, Moonies and their ilk'. So he has invented a category, 'people who believe in religion', and then chosen two incongruous examples. In what respect are nuns supposed to resemble Moonies? What sort of 'ilk' is that?

Presumably he means that religious messages can get distorted in transmission. Of course they can. So can any sort of message, including messages about Darwinism or atheism. The Christian Church (and other religious organizations) have clung very close to their sacred books to prevent that from happening. Perhaps they have clung too closely, because that causes problems too; but it is difficult to find any logical basis for Richard Dawkins' violent and illogical language. He tells readers that there are 'gangs of parasites' with collective names such as Roman Catholicism or voodoo – another deliberately incongruous coupling. The 'symptoms of infection' by the 'virus' are that the 'patient' develops convictions that do not owe anything to evidence or reason; makes a positive virtue of the fact that there is no evidence; and the 'sufferer' behaves intolerantly to members of rival faiths.[32]

He is simply saying – repeatedly – that religious ideas replicate, 'like' genes or natural viruses or infections or computer viruses. But there is no basis for comparison, and the replication of genes, natural viruses, infections and computer viruses involve very different processes, as he must know. The transmission of genes requires a male parent and a female parent, and the creation of a new person with genes from both. Viruses are invasive, simply transferred from one person to another, and as any medical handbook will confirm, their transmission is quite different from that of infective bacteria. A 'computer virus' is an electronic means of wrecking other people's computer programs. A scientist who professes the Public Understanding of Science really must know the difference between these four processes, particularly if he is an evolutionist with an enthusiasm for computers. None of the processes has anything remotely to do with the transmission of ideas, religious or otherwise.

Natural selection – a cosmic principle?

In *The Blind Watchmaker*, Richard Dawkins makes his only attempt to grapple with the problems of creation and the order of the universe. The book is principally an attack on Paley's Watch, the argument for the existence of God developed by Archdeacon William Paley, a late-eighteenth-century natural theologian. Paley argued that one can deduce the existence of a watchmaker from the design of a watch. Therefore the study of the design of the natural order, from the movement of stars and planets to the smallest forms of life, leads to a similar deduction about the existence of God.[33] In the early years of the twenty-first century, the argument from design is still with us in various forms, but not in the terms of an eighteenth-century archdeacon. He is attacking a very easy target. Paley's Watch has often been questioned by scientists and philosophers, but seldom quite so brutally.

How does Richard Dawkins explain the wider universe? He simply applies the principle of natural selection. Our solar system – and all the many other solar systems – consist of a sun, and various bodies which orbit round it because the speed at which they travel exactly balances the pull of gravity. Those that travel faster whirl off into space. Those that travel more slowly crash into the sun.[34] Natural selection is a 'blind, unconscious, automatic process'. 'It has no purpose in mind. It has no mind, and no mind's eye. It does not plan for the future. It has no vision, no foresight, no sight at all.'[35]

He sees the evolutionary principle as a sort of blind mole burrowing through history. He says that a true watchmaker has foresight, because he designs his cogs and springs for a purpose. He can see no evidence of meaning and purpose in the universe we have.

He tries to preserve the word 'evolution' for the sole use of biologists by drawing a distinction between the one great biological principle governing the universe and 'development' in any other field; but his argument is difficult to follow, and at times distinctly confused. He argues that development is a change in the form of a single object, 'as clay deforms under a potter's hands'; but evolution is 'like a sequence of frames in a cinema film'. They have different forms, but we get an illusion of change if we project the different forms in succession. Then he says that technological progress may be evolutionary, because modern aeroplanes are not like early models, and that clothes fashions may evolve rather than develop. Is the baseball cap a new form, or a development from the bowler or the top hat? He does not appear to have a sufficient grasp of semantics to follow this line of argument, and in fact, he gets tired of it after half a page, saying, 'I am not going to get into that argument now.'[36]

The study of continuities and discontinuities in particular strands of human affairs through the centuries occupies theologians, historians, archaeologists and many other specialists for their whole lives, but Richard Dawkins is concerned only to save the precious word 'evolution' for biology, and to trivialize any other kind of study. Many academics have an enthusiasm for their own professional subject, but few take it to the lengths of trying to obliterate all the other fields of scholarship. When he does look beyond biology, he does not turn to scholarship. He turns to science fiction.

Science and science fiction

Douglas Adams, the author of *The Hitch-Hiker's Guide to the Galaxy*,[37] was Richard Dawkins' close friend. Anyone who has read *HHGG*, as the fans call it, will understand how much they had in common. Douglas Adams had a good background in science and computer engineering, and Richard Dawkins was fascinated by the television series in the late 1970s. He had an ambition to write a science fiction novel himself when he was young. He wrote Douglas Adams a fan letter, and that was the beginning of a friendship which ended only when Douglas Adams died very suddenly in California in 2001 at the age of 47. In *A Devil's Chaplain*, Richard Dawkins includes both his obituary, 'Lament for Douglas', written for the *Guardian* within 24 hours of Douglas Adams' death, and the eulogy which he subsequently delivered at the memorial service in St Martin-in-the-Fields.

One might be surprised that he was prepared to attend the

service, and that Douglas Adams, who shared his atheism, had an Anglican funeral; but the Church is a tolerant institution.

Douglas Adams and Richard Dawkins both thought that the world was 'a thing of utter inordinate complexity and richness and strangeness that is absolutely awesome'.[38] They had a similar enthusiasm for Darwin's *On the Origin of Species*, for computers, for a 'love affair with science', and they had the same offbeat sense of humour. Their thinking was so close that Richard Dawkins has several times been driven to deny belief in the Infinite Impossibility Drive, a literary device that got Douglas Adams' heroes out of a tight situation more than once.

HHGG and the subsequent books in the series are basically black humour, and tinged with despair. Planet Earth is destroyed to make way for a space bypass. The last Earthman is an ape-descendant named Arthur Dent, who escapes and travels the universe. On another planet, he and his companions discover a mega-computer is built over generations to give the answer to 'Life, the Universe and Everything', but the answer is meaningless, because nobody knows what the question was. There are glancing references to Christianity: a man who worked out how to get people to be nice to one another is said to have been nailed to a cross for it. At the end of *So Long, and Thanks for All the Fish*, the weary travellers meet a man who turns everything inside out, a sort of Christ figure, and then journey to the mountains, where they find only a crumbling and indecipherable message, 'Sorry for the inconvenience'. God has given up and gone away. It is all very amusing, but it is also very sad.

Restricted vision and symbolic burkas

Towards the end of *The God Delusion*, Richard Dawkins has a section evidently written with considerable emotional force, entitled 'The Mother of All Burkas'.[39] He detests the burka (to use the usual form of the Arabic word: there is no English equivalent). He says: 'One of the unhappiest spectacles to be seen on our streets today is the image of a woman swathed in shapeless black from head to toe, peering out at the world through a tiny slit.' He uses the burka as a symbol of the restricted vision he attributes to non-scientists, and insists that only science can make us aware of the immensity and complexity of the universe: 'We look through a narrow slit in the electro-magnetic spectrum . . . what science does for us is to open the window.' This seems to contradict his earlier assertion that our understanding of the world is limited because of our descent from African apes:

> We live near the centre of a cavernous museum of magnitudes, viewing the world with sense organs and nervous systems that are equipped to perceive and understand only a small middle range of sizes, moving at a middle range of speeds. We are at home with objects ranging in size from a few kilometres (the view from a mountain top) to a tenth of a millimetre (the point of a pin).[40]

Most scientists will agree that the view of the world revealed to us by modern technology is beyond our present comprehension, and there may be many phenomena which we can observe or deduce, but will never fully understand; but Richard Dawkins' burka seems to have a particularly narrow slit, since all he can see through it is the process of natural selection and the African savannah of his childhood.

Key points

- Richard Dawkins' early experiences in East Africa, his training as a biologist, his fascination with computers and his love of science fiction all contribute to his focus on the natural world on our planet.
- He is an atheist, and can find no meaning or purpose in the universe other than the process of natural selection.
- He describes himself as a Darwinist, but he extends the concept of 'the survival of the fittest' far beyond Darwin, and ignores Mendel's contribution to modern genetics.
- Though he confesses to 'a sense of wonder' about the universe, he has no interest in the current areas of scientific discovery, and considers all other areas of scholarship, including theology, as a waste of time and effort.
- He complains that non-scientists have restricted vision, but his own range of vision is unusually narrow.

2

Out of the Cosmic Soup

Most scientists accept that the best theoretical model we have for the origin of the universe, based on our present state of knowledge, is the Big Bang; but the proposition that the Big Bang was the first step in the creation of the universe is not empirical science of the kind that can be observed, tested and confirmed by scientific method. There was no one around at the time with a stopwatch, and the experiment cannot be repeated. Big Bang theory is not what you might call 'fact', like 'The earth turns on its own axis every 24 hours'. There are still major problems to be solved.

Richard Dawkins accepts the Big Bang, but he is rather testy about it. He spells it without capital letters – big bang – and he reminds his readers that Professor Fred Hoyle, who invented the term in the late 1930s, did so 'in derision'; but he seems to accept the general proposition, which is supported by both astrophysics and particle physics. He refers repeatedly to 'the primaeval soup', in which two small particles accidentally collided, and set up a fireball of radiation, infinitely dense, which exploded in a nanosecond (that is, a small fraction of a second). This explosion is thought to have evolved into atoms that multiplied and developed, and eventually produced the universe, the solar system, Planet Earth and us. Some scientists still maintain that the whole thing happened rather more slowly, say over several million years.

Big Bang theory tells us how the universe may have started,

but offers no clues as to why, or who created it. Mathematical calculations about how long the explosion took tell us absolutely nothing about what caused it. According to Richard Dawkins and other atheists, nobody created it. The cosmic soup did not require a cosmic chef.

In Bill Bryson's *A Short History of Nearly Everything*, which is on every bookstall, the problem of a First Cause is dismissed breezily: 'It seems impossible that you can get something from nothing, but the fact that once there was nothing and now there is a universe is evident proof that you can.'[1]

Bryson is very impressed by the idea that the Big Bang probably took only 10^{-43} of a second – 10 to the minus 43rd. That is, a tiny fraction of a decimal point represented by a minus sign followed by 42 noughts and a 1. He writes it out in full, taking up nearly a whole line of print; but Bill Bryson is not a scientist. He is a journalist and a travel writer. He says he spent three years in research for the *Short History*, and that seems very likely, as he clearly put in a great deal of effort, quotes a great many sources, and gets the basic facts right; but he goes for the headline, and omits the qualifications which scientists, more cautious, add to it.

How long the creation of the universe took is much less important than the question of what caused it. To contend that it was accidental is very limited thinking. An accident to what? Accidents do not happen to nothing. In ordinary human experience, a man falls off a ladder, a car hits another car, a cliff crumbles. If the universe began accidentally, there must have been some sort of activity going on before the accident which had unintended consequences. If Richard Dawkins says that the universe originated in two particles, where did the particles come from? That is not a scientific explanation. What went BANG in that first fraction of a second? Who or what made it happen?

The only answer in scientific terms seems to be that it was

a Singularity. This is what scientists call something that they recognize, but cannot account for by what they currently understand of the laws of science. In plain English, the answer is 'We don't know'.

In his discussions with Oxford and Cambridge theologians, Richard Dawkins records that 'time and time again' they 'returned to the point that there has to be something rather than nothing'; that there must have been a first cause of everything, and we might as well give it the name God. Keith Adams, Regius Professor of Divinity in the University of Oxford, told him that the elegant solution to the problems of creation is the existence of God;[2] but Richard Dawkins rejects this on the grounds that creation is not simple: creation is very complicated. He prefers to believe in an accident, or, as he puts it, a fluke or a coincidence. It seems like a miracle, but he insists that coincidences do happen – even, it seems, to a couple of unexplained stray particles in the middle of nowhere.[3]

Religious views of eminent scientists

In one passage in *The God Delusion*, Richard Dawkins claims that most eminent scientists are also atheists, with the implication that he is in a position to speak for the whole of science: he alleges that Einstein, Stephen Hawking, and the Astronomer Royal, Martin Rees, are all atheists;[4] but this claim is not supported by their published comments on the subject.

Albert Einstein's thinking was very complex. He was plagued by reporters who wanted to know his views on God, and he gave them all sorts of different answers, some of them mischievous when they got tiresome; but he was a Jew, and Jews do not entirely lose touch with their religious past. Richard Dawkins warns readers against 'cherry-picking' from Einstein's many views – and then proceeds to do just that, selecting the ones that suit his argument. Einstein produced a paper in 1939 in which he was explicit about his views on science and religion.[5] In it, he says: 'The highest principles for our aspirations and judgements are given to us in the Jewish-Christian religious tradition . . . Are we not all children of one Father, as is said in religious language?'

Einstein also said, 'Religion without science is blind; science without religion is lame.'[6] No atheist would say that. When the first atomic bomb was dropped and Einstein said 'God does not play dice', he meant what he said. He spent most of his later years opposing the development of the bomb.

Stephen Hawking's celebrated ending to *A Brief History of Time* (1988) involved a discussion on the fact that recent findings in astrophysics and recent findings in particle physics do not fit together, and the comment that if scientists could find the link between the whole universe and the tiny particles of matter of which it is made, 'we should know the mind of God'. That may have been just a literary flourish. The last sentence of a book, breaking the contact between author and reader, is always difficult to frame. When taxed by reporters, he said he was agnostic on religious matters – which was fair enough, because the subject was beyond the scope of his data.

Martin Rees is the Astronomer Royal, and also President of the Royal Society. Richard Dawkins asked him outright about his beliefs, and reports that he replied that he is 'an unbelieving Anglican' who goes to church 'out of loyalty to the tribe'.[7] If Martin Rees actually said that, it seems likely that it was because he did not want to discuss the issue. His views are well known from his own work. In the introduction to *Before the Beginning* (1997), he says that Stephen Hawking ('or maybe his editor') thought that a mention of God would double the sales, and that he had no intention of doing the same:

In that respect, I shall not follow Stephen's lead. Scientists' incursions into theology can be embarrassingly naïve or dogmatic. The implications of cosmology for these realms of thought may be profound, but diffidence prevents me from venturing into them.[8]

In December 2004, Martin Rees made two major television presentations on the problems of cosmology, entitled *What We Still Don't Know*, on Channel 4. He ended by facing the camera and saying, 'We were no accident waiting to happen.'

Richard Dawkins also quotes Carl Sagan as an atheist; Sagan, the American author of *Cosmos* (1980) and *Pale Blue Dot* (1995), died in 1996. He was certainly a sceptic. He thought that, though there were obviously laws governing the universe, 'it does not make much sense to pray to the law of gravity'. It seems that he could not see the difference between praying to the law and praying to the Law-maker. but he was a popularizer rather than an original thinker. Few scientists would rank him with Einstein, Hawking and Martin Rees.

Richard Dawkins has a great deal to say about genes, but rarely mentions geneticists. There are hardly any references in his books to the basic research on DNA, carried out by Francis Crick and James Watson and their team at the Cavendish Laboratories at Cambridge from the 1950s on.[9] He did, it seems, question James Watson ('my friend Jim Watson') about his religious beliefs. Watson said that he found it embarrassing if religious scientists argued from revelation, and when pressed, said that he was more interested in lunch than in ultimate purpose.[10] It is understandable that any scientist, if pounced on by Richard Dawkins (perhaps after a long conference session) and asked 'Do you believe in God? Yes or no?', might not give the matter his or her full attention.

James Watson's ground-breaking book *The Double Helix*, published in 1999, is not even listed in the bibliography of *The God Delusion*. There are no references, either, to the huge international Human Genome Project, set up in 1992 and now at the end of a 15-year programme. Professor Francis Collins, the Director of the US National Human Genome Institute, does get a brief mention: he has become a Christian, and is the author of a book entitled *The Language of God* (2006). In it, he explains that he was an atheist until he was 27, but that he became interested in faith when he was a medical student. Some of his patients, even with the most terrible and terminal diseases, found that their religion gave them strength. When he started work in genetics, and worked on the human genome, that gave him a sense of awe, because it was so intricate and so elegantly designed. He resisted belief in God for years. All his scientific training seemed to be against it; but then he went walking in the mountains, and the sheer splendour of the creation hit him. He began to realize that scientists and believers were talking different languages, and engaged in a dialogue of the deaf, but they were concerned with the same phenomena.

To be fair to Richard Dawkins, he may not have read *The Language of God* before he completed *The God Delusion*, since the books were published in the same year; but when he wrote it, he was certainly aware of Francis Collins' conversion, and he has very little to say about it. His only comment is that, 'as in Britain', such examples of religious belief in scientists 'stand out for their rarity, and are a subject of amused bafflement to their peers in the academic community'.[11] It seems that, having attempted to claim that Einstein, Stephen Hawking and Martin Rees are atheists, he is trying to create a picture of them all standing together being baffled and amused by Francis Collins. This is frankly 'spin'. The facts do not warrant such an interpretation, and one expects the only Professor of the Public Understanding of Science to stand by the facts.

A flawed survey

In *The God Delusion* Richard Dawkins reproduces the findings of a social survey to support his contention that most scientists are atheists: 1074 Fellows of the Royal Society were canvassed by e-mail to discover their religious opinions,[12] and he gives the results in detail. There was a 26 per cent response rate, of whom 213 'strongly disbelieved', and only 12 'strongly believed', our of a total of 279. The questionnaire seems to have involved a Likert Scale: a five-point scale running from 'strongly disbelieve' through 'disbelieve', 'don't know', 'believe' and 'strongly believe'. All we can infer about the 54 whose views are not recorded is that they opted for one of the three middle categories.

In terms of the methodology of social surveys, this is not convincing evidence. In fact, it is not evidence at all. A 26 per cent response rate means that we only know the views of 279 people out of 1074. Of the total, 795 (74 per cent) did not reply at all, and the only data we have on them is that they failed to answer the e-mail. Any first-year social science student knows that a survey that draws less than a 50 per cent response rate is useless.

The methodology of this survey is badly flawed. Surveys of religious opinion are difficult to administer and to analyse. It is not just a matter of firing off 'Do you believe? Yes or No', and expecting to get sensible answers. No social scientist would ask such a sensitive question by e-mail. The subject requires face-to-face interviewing, a skilled interviewer and a bank of questions to tackle the subject in different ways. The sample base was inadequate, because people without e-mail addresses were excluded. Since the Royal Society is a scientific body, there may not have been many, but there is no information on how many. The sampling frame and the response rate were so inadequate that the results ought to have gone straight into the waste paper basket without further investigation.

Recent discoveries in cosmology

Scientists of the calibre of Albert Einstein, Stephen Hawking and Martin Rees have a much wider frame of reference than Richard Dawkins. If we are to consider the cause of the creation of the universe, we have to go far beyond our small world. In cosmological terms, we are temporary residents on the cooling crust of a little ball of fire that turns on its own axis every 24 hours. A smaller, dead world circles round it every 4 weeks or so, and the pair circle round the sun every 365¼ days, thus causing trouble for the people who make calendars. Once we begin to study the universe beyond our own solar system, our time system, and all the calculations we base on our understanding of time, are no longer reliable.

Isaac Newton, who discovered gravity in the seventeenth century, firmly separated space and time, and we had to wait for Albert Einstein to rejoin them in the concept of the space–time continuum. Einstein concluded by sheer mathematics, without the aid of a telescope or a computer, that space and time were related, and that the space–time continuum is curved. His five seminal papers on Special Relativity, published in 1905, completely changed the basic principles of physics, but raised many fresh questions that physicists are still trying to answer.

In *A Brief History of Time*, and *The Universe in a Nutshell*, Stephen Hawking explains more recent thinking about time. He has updated Einstein's work on space–time relativity with reference to many more recent studies. He says that Einstein's postulates still hold: all later scientists have done is to add 'a few ribbons and bows'. What he calls 'The Shape of Time' is complex. It seems that it is not a railway track or an ever-rolling stream: it has loops and branches, and possibly worm-holes. It must have had a beginning, and it must have an end, but we know absolutely nothing about either.

In recent years, enormous progress has been made in astro-physics by means of the Hubble Space Telescope, satellites and sophisticated technology. We are all rather shocked by what we can see beyond the hills and the trees. As *The Hitch-Hiker's Guide* informed us helpfully, 'the universe is mind-bogglingly big'. The light from our sun, 90 million miles away, takes 8 minutes to reach the earth. Light from some parts of the Milky Way, our own galaxy, takes thousands of years of our time to reach us. Beyond that, there are other galaxies. The average distance between major stars in space is estimated to be over 30 million billion kilometers. There may be anything from 100 million to 400 million stars in our own galaxy, and that is only 1 of a 140 billion or so galaxies.[13]

Space, according to Einstein, is curved: it has a shape; it had to be created, and most astrophysicists think that it is expand-ing. The commonsense reaction is 'Into what?', but we are getting far beyond commonsense reactions. There is a point at which physics slides into metaphysics.

People who have a lifelong familiarity with the Old Testament version of the Creation may find the cosmologists' view of the universe alarming. It certainly tests the imagination. We are a long way from the comfortable security of the Psalmist who rejoiced that 'He hath made the round world so sure that it cannot be moved.'[14] This does not prove that science and reli-gion are in conflict. It merely indicates that the Psalmist knew nothing about astrophysics, which is hardly surprising, since the Psalms were composed some thousands of years ago.

Some writers on the subject of science and religion, such as John Habgood, former Archbishop of York and the scien-tists of the Vatican Observatory, are trained in both fields of study, and well qualified to draw comparisons or note differences.[15] Type 'Science and Religion' into a computer, and the search engine or library catalogue will come up with pages of relevant literature. Richard Dawkins ignores it all.

Quantum mechanics

There is an intriguing and very basic paradox: while the universe is 'mind-bogglingly big', the stuff of which it is constructed seems to be incredibly, mind-bogglingly small. We know a fair amount about atomic structure by now. The whole universe – not only our planet, but all the other stars and planets – is made up of minute particles called leptons and quarks. Leptons can exist as free particles, but quarks cannot, so we can only infer their existence when they are in combination with leptons or some other particle. It seems that scientists can create leptons and quarks in so-called matter and anti-matter pairs, but the quarks almost instantly decay or combine with something else.

We cannot create atoms, though we know how to split them and manipulate them; and we cannot destroy them, either. It seems that those two original particles developed the capacity to combine in increasingly complex ways. Quantum theory is the study of the constituent parts of atoms, and their behaviour. They are held together and made to combine by the force of gravity, and by some other element that physicists do not understand. They call it 'invisible glue' or 'dark energy'. It emits neither light nor radiation, so that it cannot be observed or measured. They only know that it is there because the force of gravity cannot alone account for the energy with which atoms combine. So they are dealing with something that they cannot see, and inferring its existence only by the absence of any other explanation.

The main question in this field is 'What is matter?' Matter is extremely complex, and we do not know what it is. Microphysicists are currently studying molecular particles of matter so tiny that the head of a pin could hold a trillion of them, in an attempt to isolate its ultimate component. We know that quarks and leptons form themselves into complex 'families' or patterns, and are sometimes manifest as 'mass' – that is, very tiny bits of matter – sometimes as 'waves', and sometimes as wave-like particles or particle-like waves, according to Heisenberg's Uncertainty Principle.

Richard Dawkins is not the only person to find Heisenberg's proposition perplexing. He says:

> We are asked to believe that a single quantum behaves like a particle in going through one hole rather than another, but simultaneously behaves like a wave in interfering with a non-existent copy of itself if another hole is opened through which that non-existent copy could have travelled if it had existed.[16]

In *Unweaving the Rainbow*, he says that the conclusions of quantum theory are 'overwhelmingly supported by experimental evidence to a stupefyingly convincing number of decimal places', but he finds them 'so alien to the evolved human mind that even professional physicists don't understand them in their intuitive thoughts'.[17]

The current search in particle physics is for the Higgs boson, which is too small to be seen, and is thought to have a life of only a few milliseconds. The Large Hadron Collider, 17 miles long, and constructed under the Franco-Swiss border near Geneva, is now the centre of attempts to accelerate and smash particles, and identify the Higgs boson. It currently employs 7,000 scientists of many nationalities. The Higgs boson may turn out to be a property of something else rather than a particle or a wave; it may turn out to be a pair of particles, or it may contain something even smaller, less visible and shorter-lived. It may not exist at all.

In *The Blind Watchmaker*, Richard Dawkins writes, 'many of us have no grasp of quantum theory, or Einstein's theory of general and special relativity, but that does not lead us to *oppose* these theories.'[18] However, he shows little interest in these findings, which are now the subject of very large international research projects. He describes the ideas as 'queer' or 'weird', and comments that 'Modern physics teaches us that there is more to truth than meets the eye, or than meets the all too limited human mind, evolved as it was to cope with medium-sized objects moving at medium speeds through medium distances in Africa.' Evidently we are back with the chimpanzees on the savannah. He thinks there are 'profound and sublime mysteries', and that 'there may be some deep questions about the cosmos that are forever beyond the reach of science'.[19] He thinks that our minds are not equipped to handle very improbable events. He admits that events that seem improbable to us may 'turn out to be inevitable', but that leads him into science fiction rather than metaphysical speculation. He is not prepared to consider 'the God hypothesis' under any circumstances.

Genetics

As noted earlier, recent developments in the field of genetics have been so extensive and have upset so many accepted ideas that Francis Collins, arguably the most eminent geneticist of his generation, has become a Christian, and has written a book to explain why. What do we now know about genetics, apart from what Richard Dawkins tells us about selfish genes?

Human beings, like the rest of the created world, are composed of atoms: strings of genes that form genomes. Each of us has something like 35,000 or 40,000 genes in double helix structures. Genomes are capable of replication (hence Dolly the sheep and the current debate about 'designer' babies). It seems that 99.9 per cent of our genetic structure is the same for everybody – black and white, male and female, millionaires and starving children; but the odd 0.1 per cent makes an enormous difference. The genes mutate. DNA analysis shows that no two human beings are identical. We can now trace heredity over many generations, thus greatly aiding crime detection and solving the mystery of whether Anna Anderson really was the Grand Duchess Anastasia once for all. That was a case in which DNA analysis really did put an end to a lot of wishful thinking.

Geneticists cannot create life, though they have learned how to manipulate DNA, chromosomes and semen in laboratories. Apparently human beings took something like 4 billion years to evolve from the simplest life forms. A human being (any human being) is the product of some 10,000 trillion trillion atoms in a particular and unique combination.

Richard Dawkins does not appear to be particularly impressed by the uniqueness of every single human being past, present and future. Nor is he impressed by the fact that geneticists cannot create life. He thinks that there is no insuperable obstacle, and that the problems will probably be resolved in a few years' time. He talks in *The Blind Watchmaker* of 'a supersaturated solution of something like hypo' being 'eager to crystallise out of solution', and says it 'lacks only a vital ingredient' that he calls 'power'.[20] He is not really interested in whether this 'vital ingredient' is ever identified or not: he regards human beings as carbon compounds – like diamonds or lumps of limestone, but less durable. He suggests that, since we are perishable carbon compounds, computer parts (which are made of silicon, a more lasting carbon compound than human flesh), may have a better future than the human race. This is common talk in the field of computer science, where enquirers are told seriously that computers can 'think', and are better at replication than human beings. There is a whole field of discussion called 'Biocomputing' based on these premises.

Ultimate explanations

Physical scientists all over the world are searching for the answers to increasingly complex questions – and for the factors that will bring cosmology, quantum mechanics and genetics into a common framework. The goal is the development of a Grand Theory of Everything that will unite our understanding of General Relativity with our current knowledge of quantum mechanics. At present, as Stephen Hawking has explained in some detail, these two lines of speculation simply do not mesh. For a few decades, the answer seemed to lie in super-string theory, which is concerned with infinitely tiny one-dimensional massless vibrating coils of energy thought to be 100 billion billion times smaller than the proton in an atom.[21] Some quantum theorists think that they can infer the existence of super-strings; but if they do exist, they are so tiny that we have no hope of ever isolating them or testing them. That would require a particle accelerator at least the size of the earth.

In the *HHGG* series, Douglas Adams developed the idea that Planet Earth had been designed by intelligent beings on another planet, but he did not venture to speculate on where the universe as a whole came from. His great computer which was expected to find the answer to 'Life, the universe and everything' was constructed by another computer. Richard Dawkins seems to think on similar lines. Many astrophysicists, including the Astronomer Royal, Martin Rees, have at least considered the possibility of a Great Computer in the Sky, which designed everything we know and can observe; but this proposition takes us back into the realms of science fiction – or metaphysics. Anyone who uses a computer knows that you can only get out of it what has been fed into it. It needs not only an intelligent observer, but an intelligent engineer, an intelligent programmer and an intelligent operator. A computer cannot think or feel or originate: it can only associate and replicate. If there is a Great Computer in the Sky, there must be a Great Computer Engineer who created the computer. In other words, God.

While most physicists are cautious about discussing the universe in computer language, many will concede, with Martin Rees, that our world appears to be 'fine-tuned' to make human life possible. On earth, for example, if the pull of gravity were stronger, we would all fall flat on our faces. If it were weaker, we would all be floating above the surface. The mix of gasses in the air has to be just right to enable us to breathe, otherwise we would suffocate. Someone or something designed it all, though there is no scientific evidence to determine who or what. Paul Davies, a physicist with an international reputation, tackles this issue in *The Goldilocks Enigma* (2006), the latest in a series of books which attempt to make sense of scientific discoveries. He is prepared to consider religious explanations for the universe as well as non-religious ones. In 1995, he was awarded the Templeton Prize, a British book award, for *The Mind of God* (1993). Richard Dawkins is clearly irritated by this award. He mentions the Templeton Prize no less than five times in *The God Delusion*, noting that it is a very large prize (it was set up to be 'two orders of magnitude larger than the Nobel Prize'), and asserting that 'Templeton's money corrupts science'.[22] He does not list Paul Davies' books in his bibliography.

In *The Goldilocks Enigma*, Paul Davies comes to wide-ranging and thoughtful conclusions. He sets out seven different positions on the question of the origin of the universe current among his fellow scientists, pointing out that, in even considering the subject, they are moving beyond their professional expertise, and relying on their general world-view. Many of them resist doing this. Often the discussion 'slides well beyond the comfort of most scientists'.[23]

The seven different explanations are as follows:

1 'The absurd position': there is no design, no God, no explanation. Life has somehow happened, and we might as well get on with studying it.

2 The 'self-explaining universe' or Bill Bryson theory: evidently the universe is possible, because here it is.

3 The 'fake universe' theory: human life is simply a holograph – 'an ingeniously contrived reality show'. This appears to be a development from 'Biocomputing'. Those who hold this view conclude that if human life is unreal, there is little point in trying to figure it out. They do not appear to ask who designed the holograph.

4 The 'life principle' or Richard Dawkins theory: the universe began from nothing, or almost nothing, and we can study its evolution.

5 The 'multiverse' theory: many universes have been created, but as far as we know, our planet is the only one that is biofriendly, and permits human life. Apparently this explanation attracts string theorists.

6 The 'unique universe' theory: there is a deep underlying unity in different phenomena if only we can be clever enough to frame it mathematically. This sounds like the Stephen Hawking theory.

7 The theory of Intelligent Design. This has nothing to do with the Creationists' use of the term 'Intelligent Design',

which is considered in Chapter 4. What scientists mean by the term is that there is a designer behind the design, a law-giver behind the laws of science, and a cosmic chef behind the cosmic soup. As Martin Rees says, 'We were no accident waiting to happen.'

The first six positions either involve an infinite regression of causes, or simply dodge the question of the designer: the cosmic chef, the law-maker, the computer engineer. Only the concept of an intelligent designer fits the facts. It is notable that, when they come up against the frontiers of knowledge, even the most sceptical scientists often stop blinding their audience with mathematical formulae and enormous numbers, and turn to religious language. The Higgs boson (which may or may not exist) is known as the 'God Particle'. The elusive 'Theory of Everything' is known as 'the search for the Holy Grail'.

We might ask why, if scientists have found evidence of 'fine-tuning' in the conditions in which we live, if they conclude that the creation of the universe was not accidental, and that it must have been designed by a super-intelligence, they are so reluctant to come out into the open and say so.

The discussion does indeed slide beyond their comfort. When asked in serious discussion what worries them about religious solutions, they tend simply to say 'the baggage'. By this they mean the sacred books, the formulas of belief, the weight of tradition. Scientists are future-oriented, attempting to extend the boundaries of knowledge. Their field of study has changed so dramatically in recent years that most of them have little time for history: the history of science is mostly the story of outworn beliefs and discarded theories. Their professional disciplines do not extend to the why of human existence, only to the how, and they have to be very clear about where knowledge ends and where speculation begins. When they are asked to think in religious terms, they often describe themselves as agnostics, because there is so much in the universe that they simply do not understand. Many of them flinch at calling the super-intelligence 'God', because they think that term carries so many questionable assumptions. Most of them know little about recent findings in theology, or theologians' attempts to come to terms with scientific discovery. They tend to be alienated by those whom Nancy Mitford once called 'The sort of people who talk about God as though his name were Godfrey, and they were privileged to abbreviate it'. That is very off-putting to anyone with a scientific education.

Scientists have their record of saints and martyrs. The mould-breakers who challenge the conventional wisdom of the preceding centuries have always run into opposition, and they can cite many instances of persecution by the Church: Copernicus, who was so afraid to tell the world that the earth went round the sun that he only published his work on his deathbed; Galileo, who was forced by the Inquisition to deny his own conclusions, and many others; but the Church is not always the agent of opposition. Charles Darwin was denied a knighthood or a peerage – perhaps because Queen Victoria never forgave him for upsetting her beloved Albert's chaplain – but the dean and chapter insisted on burying him in Westminster Abbey. The Church, clinging to its roots, has played a part in resisting new discoveries, but the resistance to new ideas is not exclusively ecclesiastical. Social scientists call it 'cultural lag': people in authority do not like to have their conventional wisdom upset. It often takes them a very long time to adjust to new perspectives. Admittedly, it takes the Vatican longer than most. As Richard Dawkins is gratified to tell his readers, the Polish Pope, John Paul II, finally promulgated an apology to Galileo in 1992.

Are religion and science closer today in their quest for ultimate explanations than they were in the past? That is difficult to answer. There are groups of scientists, like Richard Dawkins, who want absolutely nothing to do with religion; and there are groups of religious people, like Christian and Muslim fundamentalists, who want absolutely nothing to do with science; but there are probably more people today who understand, as Francis Collins says, that the differences are more a matter of language and frames of reference than of substance. On both sides, there is increasing acceptance of the fact that there are limits to human understanding – though we have probably not reached them yet.

An intelligent Creator?

Richard Dawkins understands the limitations of observations and enquiry in the scientific field, but he cannot tolerate mystery when it is framed in religious terms; but if, as he insists, the origin of the universe was an accident that happened to nothing, all the complex discoveries of astrophysics and quantum mechanics would be totally meaningless. They would all have happened by chance, out of whirling atoms that came from nowhere. So who invented atoms? Come to that, who invented chance? All the evidence is that there is Mind – Intelligence – Purpose behind the physical universe.

In *The God Delusion*, Richard Dawkins says, 'God almost certainly does not exist. That is the main conclusion of the book so far.'[24] This is not quite the spirit of all those macho statements about 'standing tall to face the far horizon', but it is close enough. He chooses to caricature the debate about a First Cause by citing what he calls 'Pascal's Wager'.[25] The *abbé* Pascal (another religious character: how he dislikes them all) came to the conclusion that in strictly logical terms, the proofs for the existence of God and the proofs for the non-existence of God were equally plausible; but this was not a wager. Blaise Pascal was a seventeenth-century philosopher and mathematician who spent many years in calculating the mathematical probabilities. He decided that if God did not exist, human life was meaningless; but if God did exist, it had meaning and purpose. Having come to this conclusion, he determined to live by it: he entered a Jansenist monastery. Richard Dawkins' comment that 'Pascal's Wager could only be an excuse for *feigning* belief in God' bears no relation to the facts.

At the end of Douglas Adams' *So Long, and Thanks for All the Fish*, the last of the *HHGG* series and perhaps the least successful, the reader learns about the deity who created the world, but just gave up when it got into a muddle, and went away. This is more than a figment of a science fiction writer's imagination. There is an ancient myth that used to be told along the Silk Road, from Xian in China to Antalya in Turkey, about the *deus otiosus*, the god who created the world, then just shrugged and went off, leaving the human race to its own miserable concerns. None of the world's major religions take that view. They all believe that God is involved in his creation; but if we want to explore the idea that God cares what happens to the human race, we will have to look beyond the pure sciences for evidence.

Looking for proof

Richard Dawkins is militantly unprepared to do this. If the evidence for a religious view of the world is not scientific in the sense of being observable and provable, he will have nothing to do with it – though there is a great deal in the scientific field, from the Big Bang to dark energy, which he is well aware is neither observable nor provable. Science is allowed its mysteries, religion is not. In *The God Delusion*, he says:

To suggest that the first cause, the great unknown which is responsible for something existing from nothing, is a being capable of designing the universe and of talking to a million people simultaneously is a total abdication of the responsibility to find an explanation. It is an exhibition of self-indulgent, thought-denying sky-hookery.[26]

This is a very interesting paragraph. The charge of 'sky-hookery' (another word of his own invention, presumably implying that talking about God is a tactic employed by scheming clerics who want to inveigle honest unbelievers into their toils) has been widely discussed by critics, but most of them appear to have missed the implications of the first sentence. A first cause? The great unknown? Has Richard Dawkins forgotten that he is a campaigning atheist? It sounds as though he is on the road to faith, since few if any Christians, Jews, Muslims, Buddhists and Hindus would claim full knowledge of the God they worship under different names: even the saints receive only glimpses of the divine. Perhaps he is half-way there? But, having accepted the First Cause, he then promptly denies that 'the great unknown' has any interest in or contact with the creation. Here he parts company with the faithful, who are able to believe that the Intelligence capable of creating this tremendous universe, master of the unimaginably large and the infinitesimally small, creator of millions of unique individuals on our one small planet, maintains and sustains it, and can listen to any number of them simultaneously. He seems to have forgotten that our time-frame only applies to our solar system, not to the whole universe.

If religious believers have some difficulty in proving the existence of God, it is considerably less than Richard Dawkins has in proving the non-existence of God, because it is impossible in philosophical terms to prove a negative. It simply cannot be done. You can (given the evidence) prove that a positive statement is wrong, but it is not possible to prove that a negative statement is right, because there is no evidence. In *A Devil's Chaplain*, he does his best to overcome this disadvantage by quoting Bertrand Russell. That philosopher is quoted as saying of the existence of God:

> We must be equally agnostic about the theory that there is a china teapot in elliptical orbit around the sun. We can't disprove it. But that doesn't mean that the theory that there is a teapot is on level terms with the theory that there isn't.[27]

This is called 'the Celestial Teapot analogy'. On first hearing, it sounds very reasonable; but it is not reasonable, and Bertrand Russell, who was not above playing tricks on his admirers, must have known that perfectly well. It is another of those 'Just as . . .' false-analogy propositions in which Richard Dawkins so often indulges. In what respect does God – any concept of God – resemble a teapot, celestial or otherwise? We would not compare Richard Dawkins with a performing flea on the flimsy grounds that both ride bicycles.

Through the ages, people have looked for absolute proof of the existence of God. Some have pursued the idea of the Holy Grail, looked for relics of the True Cross, put their faith in miracles worked by saints' bones or even grislier relics. Perhaps we are not given that kind of proof, any more than we are given a simple explanation of how the universe works; but in terms of scientific enquiry, the proposition that the supreme Intelligence exists is considerably better supported than the proposition that the entire universe is the result of a fluke or a coincidence. If we ask what that supreme Intelligence is like, that is another question, to be pursued in other fields of learning with the same kind of rigorous integrity which scientists claim.

44

Key points

- The Big Bang is the best explanation we have of the origin of the universe.
- This does not imply that the beginning was accidental – in Richard Dawkins' terms, a fluke or coincidence.
- The eminent scientists whom he quotes as atheists do not share his anti-religious views: they recognize the boundaries of scientific enquiry, and are often reluctant to venture beyond them.
- Richard Dawkins has little to say about recent discoveries in astrophysics, quantum mechanics or genetics. These are the disciplines at the cutting edge of scientific discovery in the early twenty-first century.
- Scientists and theologians frequently debate the same issues, but in different language. In both fields, it is recognized that the scope and grandeur of the universe are beyond our comprehension.
- The question of whether the universe has a First Cause or an infinite regression of causes is a matter of metaphysics rather than physics.
- Of the 'ultimate explanations', the idea of a supreme Intelligence has the greatest explanatory power, and carries weight in the scientific community.
- Science cannot take us beyond this stage: but further enquiries require a methodology as rigorous as that of scientific method.

3

Asking Reasonable Questions

Richard Dawkins wrote his published letter to his daughter Juliet when she was ten years old. It is evidently of considerable importance to him, because he has published it twice, first in an American symposium and then in *A Devil's Chaplain*.[1] In the letter, he warns Juliet against 'three bad reasons for believing anything'. Their names are tradition, authority and revelation. Tradition, he says, means believing things 'simply because people have believed the same thing for centuries'. If you make up a story that isn't true, 'handing it down over any number of centuries doesn't make it any truer'. Authority is believing something because you are told to believe it by somebody important; but if the important person is wrong, that is not good enough. Revelation is a strong 'inside feeling'; but many people may have very different 'inside feelings'. If Juliet thinks her dog Pepe is dead, there is no point in having inside feelings about the matter. She must go and look at the dog. Scientists, he tells his daughter, work like detectives. They study the evidence, make observations, develop hunches and guesses, and 'suddenly they all fall into place and make sense if X is the murderer'.

This sounds like sensible advice to a ten-year-old girl. He does not tell his readers what prompted the letter. He wants to warn her against 'tradition', 'authority' and 'revelation', but it is a pity that he dismisses all literature that is not based

on observable fact so wholeheartedly. Is she not to read
Alice's Adventures in Wonderland or *The Wind in the Willows*
because they are 'not true'?

Fairy stories, legends and myths

Of course it is sensible to say that if a story has been handed
down for centuries, it may not be literally true. Children's
literature is full of stories which are not literally true, used to
evoke the powers of the imagination. At the age of ten, Juliet
would have come across fairy stories, a variety of legends
from different cultures and some of the great world myths.
Her father seems to be encouraging her to discount them all
– Cinderella, Beowulf, Greek mythology and King Arthur and
the Round Table; but fairy stories, legends and myths only
survive because they strike a chord in human experience, and
people find them worth retelling.

Fairy stories tell us about common human situations, and
give them a magical twist. We do not waste our time looking for the original Cinderella, but people told that story for
centuries because they knew about cruel sisters, vicious step-
mothers and poor little drudges who longed to go to the ball
and meet the handsome prince. Aladdin and his wonderful
lamp never existed, but there were plenty of poor young men
who longed to travel and have adventures, and looked for a
way of proving how brave and strong they were when faced
with danger. Fairy tales are mostly wish-fulfilment stories,
about individual human dilemmas and situations.

Legends, according to Carl Gustav Jung, represent human
archetypes – primordial images that recur so constantly that
they become part of general human experience.[2] He thinks
that they became genetically coded, so that they are transmitted from generation to generation by the 'collective

unconscious', but some schools of psychoanalytic theory dispute that. Legends are stories that accumulate around well-known characters, a process that Richard Dawkins calls 'Chinese Whispers'. Of course it involved an accumulation of inaccuracies in the days when most people were unable to read or write, and information was passed on by word of mouth. Legend is gossip, and frequently unbelievable.

Myth is different. Most anthropologists take the view that myth has reference to social structures and social situations, and is a tool for transmitting group experience. The stories about King Arthur and his court at Camelot are myth. By the time Malory wrote them down in the fifteenth century in the *Morte d'Arthur*, they had become a symbol of the heroic resistance of English chivalry to the forces of evil.[3] Myth needs careful interpretation to elicit its underlying meaning and function. It is not history, but it becomes part of the way we look at the world. It is important to understand the significance of myth, because there are substantial myths in both the scientific and the religious view of life – though Juliet is being warned only against the religious ones. For where do tradition, authority and revelation count for more than in Islam, the Roman Catholic Church and the extreme Evangelical movements? These forms of religious organization are clearly the targets of his attack.

Juliet is being told to make her own independent enquiries. Clearly, if she thinks her dog Pepe is dead, the thing is to go and find out, not to spin theories about it, or take someone else's word for it. If Pepe gets to his four feet and barks, he is not dead; but not all questions can be resolved in this straightforward fashion.

Do scientists work like detectives? That is a good enough explanation for a ten-year-old, perhaps; but the world of science is a good deal more complicated than the world of Poirot or Detective Columbo. Certainly scientists study the evidence and make observations where and as they can, with new and powerful tools. Of course they develop hunches and guesses, and try to test them out; but much of their work is theoretical, and based on mathematical calculations. These are fundamentally exercises in logic: if A and B are true, then C must follow. As we have seen, much advanced scientific investigation does not come up with firm answers, and science has a trail of exploded myths which were once accepted as sober fact: Harvey thought that the circulation of the blood mimicked the movement of the planets. Darwin was convinced that the menstrual flow in women was connected to the ocean tides. The current advocates of 'biocomputing' are using a machine as a model of the human brain. Possibly some of the more way-out scientific speculation about parallel universes and wormholes in space may turn out to be mythical, too.

Richard Dawkins is right in saying that the only way forward is to take a close look at the evidence, and then make one's own judgement, whether the subject is a scientific or a theological one; but he defines science as 'the search for truth,'[4] and says that faith is 'blind trust in the absence of evidence, even in the teeth of the evidence'.[5] This is not what is meant by 'faith' in theological terms or in ordinary speech.

The word 'faith' has at least three common meanings. When we talk of 'faith groups' or 'faith schools', we are referring to recognized groups of people – Christian, Jewish, Muslim and so on – who share a set of beliefs. When we talk about our own faith, we mean what we personally believe in as a result of using common sense, logic and experience. We do not mean superstition, wishful thinking, self-delusion. When we talk of 'a leap of faith', we mean what we deduce or hypothesize about the things our restricted vision prevents us from verifying.

Richard Dawkins has very little to say in his writings about philosophy. Since it is a 'meme', and not based on 'science' as he understands it, he regards the whole area of enquiry as largely irrelevant; but in *The God Delusion*, he does mention three philosophers who are generally regarded as masters of rigorous thinking: Thomas Aquinas, Immanuel Kant and Karl Popper. His comments on their work may serve as a measure of his understanding of the methodology of academic enquiry.

Thomas Aquinas and logical method

Thomas Aquinas was a Dominican scholar (another monk) who lived in the thirteenth century.[6] Why does Richard Dawkins bring him into the argument? After all, Aquinas knew nothing about the Hubble telescope and silicon chips, and he probably thought that the sun went round the earth. He attacks him because Thomist thought, as it is called, still exerts a very powerful influence in the Roman Catholic Church. In 1879, Pope Leo XIII urged Catholic philosophers to draw their inspiration from him, while developing his philosophy to meet modern intellectual needs. Philosophers such as Étienne Gilson and Jacques Maritain have analysed and publicized his ideas, so that they are still very influential in Roman Catholic theology.

Richard Dawkins cites Aquinas only to attempt to ridicule and dismiss his celebrated arguments about the existence of God. He allots three pages to this effort. The writings of Thomas Aquinas run to many volumes, and cover every aspect of Christian theology. His enquiry into the existence and nature of God occurs at a very early stage in his *Summa Theologica*, and this work alone runs to 22 large volumes. Thomas had a mind like a sledgehammer. He broke each of his topics into questions, raised objections against each question in turn, answered the objections, objected to the answers, and then answered the new objections.[7]

So what does Richard Dawkins make of this massive and thorough investigation, the product of many years of scholarly debate and literary toil? His three pages include a flippant little poem, a long discursion on Edward Lear's Nonsense Recipe for Crumboblius Cutlets, and a rather pointless anecdote about Euclid, probably remembered from his schooldays. He sweeps aside the first three proofs (God as the First Mover, God as the Efficient Cause, God as the Ground of Necessity) by refusing 'to allow the luxury of arbitrarily conjuring up a terminator'. God as the Terminator? This is another false analogy, and a rather nasty one. When he gets to the fourth proof (God as the superlative, the essence of Truth, Goodness and Beauty), he regresses to the schoolboy level:

> That's an argument? You might as well say, people vary in smelliness, but we can make the comparison only by reference to a perfect maximum of conceivable smelliness. Therefore there must exist a pre-eminently peerless stinker.[8]

He disposes very quickly of the fifth argument (Design and Purpose), since he can see no evidence of either.

If he had studied the works of Thomas Aquinas with a little more application, Richard Dawkins might have discovered that in the medieval universities, *scientia* meant all knowledge, not just the physical sciences. Learning was not chopped up into little bits of expertise with different names and competing philosophies; and it was based on logic. Thomas Aquinas started from observation of the physical world. He thought that there were two types of explanation:

> One kind goes to the root of the matter, as in natural science, when a sufficient proof is advanced to show that the velocity of astronomical motion is constant. The other is less radical, but lays down an hypothesis, and shows that the observed effects are in accordance with the supposition.[9]

He also thought that observation and logical analysis preceded faith:

> The existence of God and similar truths about him attainable by strict rationalism are not articles of faith, but preambles to them. Faith presupposes natural knowledge, even as grace presupposes nature . . . there is nothing to prevent a man from accepting as an article of belief something that can be scientifically known and demonstrated, though perchance not by him.[10]

What does Richard Dawkins make of this description of natural theology? Nothing, because he never mentions it, and perhaps never read far enough to encounter it. The curious thing is that, in spite of his blind spots and his short cuts, he claims that, like Thomas Aquinas, he believes in absolute truth:

> A lawyer or a politician is paid to exercise his passion and his persuasion on behalf of a client or a cause in which he may not privately believe. I have never done this, and I never shall. I may not always be right, but I care passionately about what is true, and I never say anything that I do not believe to be right.[11]

Aquinas pushes observation and logical deduction as far as he can, but recognizes the limits. He realizes that a full knowledge of God is beyond human grasp. Then he uses a very vivid phrase: 'The bat blinks in the blaze of the sun.'[12] The aristocratic family of Aquino lived in a remote and cavernous castle in the Apennines, between Rome and Naples. Thomas must have spent a lot of time in his childhood looking at the bats. When a bat detaches itself from its shadowy perch in a dark cave, it will sometimes blunder its way out of the darkness to take a quick look at the sunlit world outside. Bats' hideous little faces are very expressive, and one can see exactly what Thomas meant: the attraction, the repulsion, the hesitation, the sleepy incomprehension, the urge to scuttle back into the dark. That is how many people think about God: perhaps Richard Dawkins is one of them.

Religious conflict and the decline of logical thinking

When did 'faith' get separated from logic and deduction, and become primarily a matter of desperate conviction? Perhaps the process started with the cumulative experience of the Crusades, because Christians found themselves in conflict with a dogmatic faith, combined with Arab militarism, which opposed their own. From the late eleventh century to the late thirteenth century, the kings and princes of Europe, supported by the nobility and their retainers, fought to save Jerusalem and the pilgrim routes under the banner of the cross – and lost; and for another two centuries after that, the Muslim advance continued – through the Balkans, across North Africa, up through Spain and into France. It was not until the time of Ferdinand and Isabella, the Catholic kings of Spain, that the Muslim forces were driven out of Western Europe. Faced with Muslim dogma, Christians responded with Christian dogma. Faith came to be defined in words, not deeds. Ecclesiastical courts were established to try heretics, with legal procedures to decide who was a heretic and who was not. Asking questions – even reasonable questions – was held to be proof of heresy, because the Church claimed to have a complete monopoly on the answers.

The work of the Inquisition was most active in Spain, where Christians, Muslims and Jews had lived side by side in reasonable amity in places like Seville and Toledo and Salamanca for centuries. After 1479, the long lines of *Conversos* were paraded through the streets, and those who refused to 'confess', that is, to subscribe to a precise statement of Christian belief, were handed over to the civil arm for execution. Thomist thought, which had begun in free enquiry, had become a kind of intellectual straitjacket. The lively theology of the medieval schoolmen, the cut and thrust of theological debate, was simply driven underground.

The rapid spread of Protestantism in Northern Europe in the sixteenth century was a revolt against the authoritarian Church, but the Reformation coincided with the rise of the nation-state, and rulers like England's Henry VIII used it for their own ends. Sadly, the Protestant states and the Protestant theologians developed their own kind of authoritarianism, based on a literal reading of the Bible. The study of theology became a matter for assertion, not for enquiry.

Richard Dawkins writes: 'I have deliberately refrained from detailing the horrors of the Crusades, the *Conquistadores* and the Spanish Inquisition. Cruel and evil people can be found in every century and of every persuasion.'[13] The only horror to which he gives any consideration is the deaths of Nicholas Ridley, Hugh Latimer and Thomas Cranmer, burned at the stake in the reign of Mary Tudor.

The Oxford Martyrs

The three clerics – Bishop of Worcester, Bishop of Rochester and Archbishop of Canterbury respectively in the reign of Edward VI – were Protestants. The place of their execution is marked by the Martyrs' Memorial in Oxford, at the junction between St Giles and the Banbury and Woodstock Roads. Richard Dawkins must have passed it many times on his way from the Zoology Department into town. He asks how the three could 'let themselves be burned, rather than forsake their Protestant Little-Endism for Catholic Big-Endism? Does it really matter from which end you open a boiled egg?'[14]

He insists that religious conflict is unimportant; but if he treats history as a spotlight, he cannot see patterns of cause and effect. In the reign of Mary Tudor, it was very important for political reasons. The trials of Ridley, Latimer and Cranmer were show trials. The Pope and Philip II of Spain, Mary's husband, were trying to force England back into the Catholic fold. The three were imprisoned, ill treated, humiliated, continuously harangued by Spanish friars, publicly degraded and eventually burned alive in order to bring the rest of the clergy into line with the new regime.[15] Treating history as a spotlight obscures the issues and the reasons for resistance.

The execution of the Oxford Martyrs was barbarous, but many Catholics were executed by Protestants with equal barbarity. The Abbots of Glastonbury, Reading and Colchester were executed on the orders of Henry VIII.[16] Sir Thomas More and Bishop John Fisher died to ensure the compliance of the clergy to Henry VIII's Act of Supremacy.[17] Idealistic young priests like Edmund Campion and Alexander Briant hid in priests' holes, but in the end, died at Tyburn.[18] This was a tragic period in English history. Richard Dawkins does not mention any of the Catholic Martyrs, but he grieves at the 'unnecessary' deaths of Cranmer, Latimer and Ridley. 'Couldn't they cross their fingers, or whisper "not" under their breath?' he asks. They could not. He makes a stand for atheism, but he cannot understand people who made a stand for faith. He parades his own honesty. He might try to understand theirs.

Rational enquiry in early science fiction

In the time of religious conflict, people who had new ideas had to be cautious about them. If they committed their ideas to paper, it was safer to write in terms of another country or another world. The discovery of the Americas led to a search for new knowledge which came bubbling up through the Humanist movement. Thomas More, who was a very cautious Humanist, solved the problem of how to express unorthodox views by writing science fiction. *Utopia* (1516) means 'no place'. By setting his analysis in Nowhere, More was able to imagine all sorts of surprising things: a society where there was no money, everyone shared the necessary labour, and goods were communally owned; where divorce was possible (but only once) and euthanasia was permitted; and where there were women priests.

By the seventeenth century, there was a good deal of rather fanciful travel literature. One very influential work was Francis Bacon's *The New Atlantis* (1625).[19] Bacon, like More, was Lord Chancellor of England. He worked out a scheme for a scientific establishment which has led, among many other things, to Richard Dawkins' views on the supreme importance of science, and his appointment as a Fellow of the Royal Society.

Bacon was convinced that empirical investigation would be the basis of all future advances in knowledge. *The New Atlantis* was an account of a fictitious journey by ship to a strange land 'full of boscage' where the people were Christian and civilized, but far ahead of Europeans in their scientific understanding. They had a splendid college for teaching and research in many subjects – including meteorology, medicine, pharmacy, horticulture, chemistry, physics, mathematics, brewing and baking and much else, even aeronautics (in case there should be 'some degree of flying in the air' in the future). At this time, there were only two English universities, Oxford and Cambridge, and study at both was heavily weighted in favour of what Richard Dawkins calls 'memes' – history, philosophy, theology. Science had very little place there. Scientists were often forced to conduct their experiments in outhouses or private houses, and medicine was restricted to hospitals and furtive dissections. Bacon's dream, worked out in considerable detail, finally obtained a Royal Charter from Charles II in 1662, and became the Royal Society.

The New Atlantis contains most of Richard Dawkins' assumptions about the pre-eminence of the pure sciences and the relative unimportance of other branches of learning; and some of the arrogance, too. Apparently Bacon died in the cause of empirical enquiry. He got out of his coach on a bitterly cold day to examine a chicken which lay dead in the road to find out whether refrigeration by snow had kept it fresh. He caught a cold, and died of pneumonia.

The Age of Reason: Kant's exposition

Scientists became enthusiastic about what became known as 'scientific methods', but reason and logic were not fully restored to other branches of learning until the eighteenth century. Immanuel Kant,[20] Professor of Logic and Metaphysics at Konigsberg, was the author of three fundamental texts: *The Critique of Pure Reason*, *The Critique of Practical Reason* and *The Critique of Judgement*.

Richard Dawkins commends Kant for developing the principle that a rational being should never be used as a means to an end, even the end of benefitting others.[21] He concedes that Kant was a Christian, but brushes the inconvenient fact aside by saying that everyone was nominally Christian in Kant's day. Then he criticizes Kant for advocating absolute moral standards, on the grounds that 'It is pretty hard to defend absolutist morals on grounds other than religious ones,'[22] and follows with a long discussion of his own views on euthanasia, homosexuality and abortion: subjects of which Kant probably knew very little.

Having attempted the demolition of Thomas Aquinas in three pages, he has allowed Kant two and a half; but Kant developed what he called 'a Copernican revolution in philosophy', exploring and defining the nature and limits of human reason. In his time, most philosophers still assumed that truth could be defined without reference to the real world, while scientists believed only in what they could observe by means of the five senses. What they could not hear, see, taste, touch or smell did not exist. Kant argued that empirical evidence and logical analysis were both necessary in any search for truth. Where observation was possible, ideas should be tested out; but not every kind of human experience was testable. When scholars made new discoveries, they needed to use logic in order to try to fit their findings into a theoretical framework. Kant established the importance of validating what could be confirmed by 'sense' or human experience, and the equal importance of recognizing 'intelligence', which is how we order it. He understood that many questions about creation and human life were beyond the reach of observation and measurement. That was the area of metaphysics. He was well ahead of his generation in realizing that human knowledge is limited by our experience of space and time. (If only he had been able to talk to Einstein.)

Kant developed the concept of the Categorical Imperative. This is what distinguishes human beings from chimpanzees. This is what distinguishes human beings from computers. This is what makes us more than 'selfish genes'. Kant noted that each of us has an implanted sense (or as Richard Dawkins would say, is hard-wired) to know the difference between right and wrong. This does not imply rigid rules, as absolutism does: it implies the capacity to employ conscience and make value judgements. The Categorical Imperative is very similar to what Quakers call 'the Inner Light'. People who do not have this capacity used to be called 'psychopaths' or 'sociopaths', and are now defined by psychiatrists, and in law, as suffering from personality disorder. Unless they are very wealthy (and sometimes if they are) they end up in prison. Most people understand the Categorical Imperative instinctively without needing to be told by a philosopher: on television, in the supermarket, on the football field, they say 'That's not *right*'. Even children in the playground say 'That isn't *fair*'. But recognition of the Categorical Imperative would destroy Richard Dawkins' case completely. It would bring some of his arguments to a standstill.

In the two centuries since Kant, the boundary between physics and metaphysics has moved as we discover more about the physical world; but it has also become blurred. Scientists have developed theories about phenomena too vast or too small for physical measurement, while theologians have found scientific equipment to assist their enquiries. Kant's thinking is still important, because he gave a new dignity to human reason after a long period in which it was lost or devalued. People would no longer believe something simply because they were told to believe it. They wanted to think for themselves.

Karl Popper's formula for problem-solving

Of the many successors of Kant, many people rate Professor Karl Popper[23] as the most effective logician. Even Richard Dawkins respects him. In *The Selfish Gene*, he comments:

'The analogy between scientific progress and genetic evolution by natural selection has been illuminated especially by Sir Karl Popper.'[24] He seems to have reached a point where he is prepared to admit that genetic evolution is not the only form of evolution: the development of scientific ideas can also be described as 'evolution'; though he is not prepared, as Popper is, to extend this status to the development of ideas in other branches of learning.

Popper's work is not easy to read, for several reasons. He was born and grew up in Vienna, and *The Logic of Scientific Discovery* was written in German. That is a good language in which to think and write philosophy, but the ideas can be difficult to translate into English. Popper's later works are written in English, but his method of presentation is idiosyncratic. Sometimes he starts with Plato or Aristotle, and presents his own arguments as developments of theirs, and that is not very helpful to readers who lack a good grasp of Plato and Aristotle. He often uses terms in formal logic, which is shorthand for other philosophers, but quite difficult for other readers to follow. A good starting-point for reading Popper is Brian Magee's small book,[25] which explains the essentials, and will tell the reader where to go next.

Popper's writing is extensive, and contains many seminal ideas, but for the purposes of assessing Richard Dawkins' contentions, we can select his formula for investigation,[26] which is as revolutionary as Einstein's $E = mc^2$.

$$P_1 \dashrightarrow TS \dashrightarrow EE \dashrightarrow P_2$$

This is a formulaic way of saying that a research worker

1 starts with a problem (P_1);
2 proceeds to an hypothesis which can be tested, and attempts a Trial Solution (TS);

3 assesses his or her results, and proceeds to Error Elimination (EE);
4 reframes the problem (P_2).

Sometimes research produces a result which we might call FS, or Final Solution, but more often it generates a set of new problems which can be refined and used to shape new hypotheses. This process is continuous.[27]

Popper suggests that the most sensible way of proceeding with an hypothesis is not to try to confirm it, but to try to disprove it. For instance, if we take the proposition that 'All swans are white', there is no need to rush around recording white swans: we should look for a black one. When we find one, we need to check our data. Is it really a swan? Where do black swans originate? Can they mate with white swans? The original finding generates a whole host of new questions. This principle is elegant and economical, and it has saved an enormous amount of money in research costs. Research workers used to replicate existing findings over and over in the attempt to confirm them. If they can disprove a proposition, they can move on to the next problem.

Popper tells us that human beings are problem-solving animals, the only problem-solving animals. The process of discovery is open-ended, and all human knowledge is provisional. There are no ultimate solutions to the important questions. The world and our understanding of it are constantly changing. We reshape our problems, and try again, and there is always more to be found out. Only the journalists and popularizers think they can find certainty. If, as Richard Dawkins maintains, 'science is the search for truth',[28] and 'it is of the essence of science to know what we do not know. This is precisely what drives us to find out',[29] a problem-solving approach will show us the way forward.

Where do we look for problems and solutions about God?

First of all, to the Bible, beginning with the Old Testament – a topic on which Richard Dawkins has a great deal to say.

Key points

- Richard Dawkins' advice to his daughter draws a distinction between scientific investigation and faith, which he regards as based on myths.
- Myths are social constructs which require careful interpretation.
- The word 'faith' has at least three different meanings.
- The three philosophers whose work he cites all have a much more sophisticated understanding of methods of enquiry than Richard Dawkins suggests.
- The writings of Thomas Aquinas are based on logic. This approach to theological questions was common in the medieval universities, but was virtually lost in the fifteenth and sixteenth centuries, being replaced by religious orthodoxy in a time of conflict.
- Kant and his contemporaries rediscovered Reason – and the distinction between human beings and animals (which also distinguishes them from computers). Human beings have a moral sense.
- Karl Popper introduced us to the evolution of ideas, and the concept that human beings are the only problem-solving animals. He provides a useful framework for our next enquiries.

4

God of our Fathers

The first five books of the Old Testament – Genesis, Exodus, Leviticus, Numbers, Deuteronomy, known as the Pentateuch – constitute the Jewish Torah, the most revered text in Judaism. Jesus Christ frequently quoted from the Torah. In the Qur'an, the Prophet Muhammad calls it the Book,[1] and exhorts his followers to obey its teachings. All the stories we know from childhood – Adam and Eve, Noah and the Flood, Abraham, Jacob, Joseph and Moses – are part of a common heritage for Christians, Arabs and Jews. They are all People of the Book.

When Richard Dawkins writes about the Old Testament, he leaves readers in no doubt about his reactions. We have seen Dawkins the biologist, Dawkins the computer enthusiast, Dawkins the science fiction addict. Now we see Dawkins the stern moralist, turning a truly Old Testament fury on the Old Testament itself.

God in the Book of Genesis

Comments on what he calls 'the God of the Old Testament' are indexed in *The God Delusion* under such headings as 'Yahweh, deplorable character of' or 'shocking role model'. Perhaps his most explosive passage is this:

The God of the Old Testament is arguably the most unpleasant character of all fiction: jealous, and proud of it; a petty,
unjust unforgiving control freak; a vindictive, bloodthirsty
ethnic cleanser; a misogynistic, racist, infanticidal, geno-
cidal, filicidal, pestilential, megalomaniacal, sadomasochis-
tic, capriciously malevolent bully.[2]

This torrent of adjectives is followed by a number of separate
charges: Adam and Eve were punished for 'scrumping',[3] that
is, stealing apples, and the human race has been punished for
it ever since. Perhaps he scrumped apples himself when he
was a boy. He thunders, 'What kind of ethical behaviour is
it that condemns every child, before it is born, to inherit the
sin of a remote ancestor?' We might expect him to approve of
the story of Noah, who, after all, was the first conservation-
ist; but though he thinks that the story is 'charming', he finds
its morality appalling.[4] Noah and his family and sample pairs
of different species of animals are saved, but everybody else,
including all the children and the animals, is drowned in the
Flood for the sins of a few. He is outraged again by Abraham.
Christians, Jews and Muslim Arabs all regard themselves as
the Children of Abraham; but what, he asks, what would the
police and the courts make today of a man who tied his child
up and threatened him with a knife? He would be put in jail
for child abuse.[5]

It is notable that Richard Dawkins' disapproval of 'the God
of the Old Testament' and his celebrated followers is largely
confined to quotations from the book of Genesis, though he
is clearly unhappy with later references to Jewish triumphalism after battles against the Philistines, the Amalekites, the
Canaanites, the Moabites and the other marauding tribes
around them. He is, of course, aware that most theologians
do not take the early stories literally, but he may well be right
in saying that 'despite the good intentions of the sophisticated

theologian', a frightening number of people do. He quotes a Gallup Poll in which 50 per cent of Americans agreed that the Flood was 'a payback for human misdemeanours',[6] and an Israeli survey in which two-thirds of a sample of Israeli children approved of Joshua and his men slaughtering the entire population of Jericho, killing their animals and looting their possessions. He asks, are we to 'pick and choose' which bits of scripture to believe?[7] He is clearly very angry, with what he feels is a righteous anger.

What is the Old Testament?

However, he is well aware that the Bible does not speak with a single voice. 'To which book of the Bible should we turn – for they are far from unanimous,' he complains. Then he describes the Old Testament as

> just plain weird – a chaotically cobbled together anthology of disjointed documents composed, revised, translated, distorted, and 'improved' by hundreds of anonymous authors, editors and copyists, unknown to us and mostly to each other, spanning nine centuries.[8]

The Old Testament is not a single book. It is a whole library, a collection of books and sayings dating from different periods of history over several thousand years. It starts with an account of how one particular people, the Jews, thought the world was created. Other cultures have their own creation stories, but this one is the beginning of a remarkable saga. It goes on to the stories of folk heroes like Noah and Abraham and Moses, rules about how the Jews were to live, long genealogical tables in the male line (all that begetting), historical records of their kings and their battles, and summaries of the preaching of their great prophets, and records their longing for a Messiah, who will right wrongs and bring about a just society. The later material is based on written documents, but the earliest accounts come from a non-literate society. They must have been passed on by word of mouth round the camp fires for centuries before they were recorded.

The Old Testament has an internal coherence, and it tells a developing story. Richard Dawkins' repeated references to 'the God of the Old Testament' suggests that it presents only one view of God. This is not the case, The early stories are pre-history, and we cannot be precise in dating their origins.

They come from a period when the Jewish people had a very limited idea of God – they were nomadic herdsmen, moving with their flocks and defending them against other predatory tribes. They were not Oxford dons. When, through centuries of sin and suffering and exile, they settled down and developed ideas of kingship and priesthood, justice and mercy, they came to a more advanced understanding of their God; but the stories in Genesis come from people who are just beginning to develop moral and theological understanding. At first, their ideas about God were very elementary, but they were trying to work out some fundamental questions: how did the world begin? Why are there two kinds of people, men and women? Are men superior to women? Why do we do wrong things, when we know they are wrong? Why do women give birth in pain? Why do men have to work so hard? How did murder originate? They are intelligent questions. They express basic human experience at a very deep level, and tell us about the ideas and values of this early culture as it sought to understand the nature and purpose of the Creator. This is myth – the explanation developed in an ancient pastoral society of what people could see and experience for themselves. It is a starting-point. It can tell us a great deal about who they were, and how they thought, but it only has significance if it is read with understanding.

Richard Dawkins begins at the beginning, with book 1, chapter 1. That is the way one reads a novel, not the way a scholar approaches a library of books. Nearly all his comments are on the first chapters of the book of Genesis. He has nothing to say about the book of Job, one of the most profound accounts we have of human suffering. He ignores the Psalms – 150 poems written after the Exile to Babylon – which show every approach to God from praise and thanksgiving to desperate trust in times of defeat and near-despair. He takes no interest in all the prophets, from Jeremiah to Malachi, who preach a vision of right living and social harmony. The story of the Jewish people's growing understanding of God finds fulfilment in the life and message of Christ in the New Testament; but the creation stories are simply early tribal background. To dismiss the whole of the Old Testament on the evidence of the book of Genesis is like dismissing British history on the basis of what we know about the Stone Age.

The significance of Bible myth

The first story of all – 'In the beginning, God . . .' – is a remarkable composition. Its words and its cadences were honed and refined in repeated recitation long before it was written down. In 31 verses of spare and beautiful language, it tells of the creation of the earth and the heavens and everything in them. It tells successively of the creation of order out of chaos, land and sea, plants and fruit, sun and moon, fish and fowl, cattle and creeping things, and finally human beings. Adam and Eve are given charge over the earth, and on the seventh day God rests from his labours. This is an all-powerful God, but a very human one. He gets tired with the effort of creation, and takes the seventh day off. Sometimes he gets angry, sometimes he gets jealous, sometimes he is pacified by

prayers and sacrifices. The Genesis story is not the only creation story. Richard Dawkins complains that religion seems to
be 'ubiquitous', and certainly every culture in every age seems
to have evolved its own explanation about how the world
originated; but few, if any, have the simplicity and none the
grandeur of this account.

Some creation stories start with a primeval mother, a
corn-goddess or a rice-goddess, celebrated with the changing
seasons of the year. Some start with a union between primeval
parents, who usually quarrel, or whose children quarrel with
them and assert their independence. Some rather gruesome
myths start with the dismembering of the body of a god, like
the Norse Edda, or the Indian Rigveda. There are some so-
called emergent myths, like those found among the Navajo
Indians, in which human beings develop from animals, as
they do in evolution theory.[9] In many, the themes of conflict,
sacrifice and the relationship between good and evil recur frequently. All human societies seem to feel the need to explain
their experience in these terms; and in the Bible stories, they
are developed in the stories of Adam and Eve, Cain and Abel,
Noah and the patriarchs, beginning with Abraham.

If the Genesis stories are rated as more significant than
those in other cultures, it is not only because of their literary quality. The Jews were unique in believing in one God,
instead of the many – often bloodthirsty and capricious – gods
of the surrounding peoples, and they tried to listen to what
their God taught them. They believed that this one God was
a moral being who spoke directly to them and taught them
how to behave. They learned about him by trial and error
through the centuries. They were the only people who were
really *looking* for God, and who felt that they were in relationship with him. They made mistakes, but there was a kind
of dogged simplicity and commitment to the search.

These stories are not about what we would consider moral

behaviour now, nor are they about God as theologians now understand him. By taking them at face value and then rejecting them, Richard Dawkins repeatedly misses the point: for instance, he assumes that Adam and Eve were banished from the Garden of Eden for stealing apples, and then jumps to the concept of original sin, which was attributed to this first disobedience, and asks why children should be thought to inherit their sins from their remote ancestors. His own work on genes starts from the assumption that human beings and animals do inherit genetically from their remote ancestors. How else could he describe the human race as 'ape descendants'? The story of Adam and Eve and the apple may be myth, but it is an excellent illustration of the operation of the selfish gene through the generations.

In the myth, the sin is not stealing an apple: it is disobeying God's command. Adam and Eve, given free will, used it to disobey God. Richard Dawkins believes in free will. He asks us to '*teach* altruism because we are born selfish'. As a university professor, he believes that people can learn. He also says 'Genes aren't us'. He knows that we have the capacity to choose.

If one insists on taking the story of Adam and Eve at face value, it is certainly possible to present God as being downright malicious. He created these two young people, and set them in the garden. Why put the apple tree (some say it was a fig tree) there in the first place? Why give Adam and Eve a sense of curiosity? Why create the snake (one of the 'creeping things') who tempted Eve? If God had intended human beings to remain in a state of primal innocence, it looks as though he could so easily have avoided the whole situation. We would not put a plate of cakes in front of a hungry child, and then say 'You'll have to leave home if you touch one'; but these pastoral people were struggling, as we all do, with problems of right and wrong, and they had a strong sense that somehow people were not behaving in the way they ought to behave. Life ought to be gentle and peaceful, but it was not. It was cruel and harsh. They developed their own explanation, and it had such power that it has come to us down the centuries.

Richard Dawkins is quite right in saying that if a father behaved to his son today as Abraham behaved to Isaac, tying him up, laying him out as a sacrifice and brandishing a knife in front of him, he would certainly end up in prison; but again, he misses the point. These ancient herdsmen did not have modern ideas about child abuse and human rights, and the story is not about the treatment of the child Isaac. It is about how Abraham learned that God did not require human sacrifices. Most of the ancient peoples of the Middle East did make human sacrifices to placate their gods. Abraham was offering God his most precious possession, his first-born son. The realization that God did not want or expect that kind of sacrifice was a big step forward in spiritual understanding.

Abraham is not a moral person by our standards. If Richard Dawkins was looking for ammunition, he might have cited his treatment of the slave-girl Hagar,[10] which would have incurred the wrath of the Child Support Agency at the very least; but this is not a story about a rejected slave-girl and her son, Ishmael. It is an attempt to explain why Israelites and Ishmaelites were so much alike, but the Ishmaelites were poorer and despised as inferior. The explanation was ingenious: both must be descended from Abraham, but with different mothers. One was the son of the proper mistress of the household, and the other merely a servant's son.

Other tribal accounts, gradually shading into history, similarly attempt to explain how things came to be the way they were: Jacob cheats his elder brother Esau out of his inheritance by impersonating him at his father's deathbed;[11] King David plots the death of Uriah the Hittite, because he coveted Uriah's wife Bathsheba.[12] The triumphalism, the determination to wipe out the surrounding tribes, is perhaps understandable: there were no national boundaries, no peacekeepers, no conferences; only the law of kill or be killed. But accepting the early parts of the Old Testament at face value means accepting the values of a very early society – slavery, concubinage, child abuse, cheating, murder and racism – all as being 'the will of God'. These stories come from people with very shaky and primitive ideas about what their God was like, and how he expected them to treat each other.

God as the Universal Father

The herdsmen who developed the early Old Testament stories conceptualized God in terms of their own understanding of the world. Inevitably, they saw him as a man – being tired on the seventh day after the effort of creation, walking in the garden in the cool of the day, annihilating his enemies, bringing disasters to punish his people for their refusal to keep faith with him. These stories were developed while they watched their cattle or sat and relaxed in the evening after sunset. They cannot have paid much attention to what the women were chattering about in their tents.

The Jewish scribes who recorded these stories later were men. The highest view they had of their God was that he was the ultimate Father, the progenitor of the whole human race. They came to learn that he was a God of justice and mercy, but they saw him as the King of Kings: they knew nothing of democracy, and nothing of gender equality. He was the archetypical old man with a gold crown and a beard sitting on a golden throne, who has come down to us from the hand of nearly every artist from early Christian times via Michaelangelo and Raphael to William Blake and beyond. These images are in every church and every art gallery in the Western world. They are so pervasive that it is still very difficult for us to get beyond them. It is less than 50 years since John Robinson, Bishop of Woolwich, published a book called *Honest to God*, in which he argued that God was not an old man with a beard. This led to him being attacked on all sides by people whose images of God had been formed by Renaissance paintings, stained-glass windows and church calendars. Commentators said that it was all very well to say that sort of thing in the privacy of a Cambridge Common Room, but not in public. Bishop Robinson's obituary in *The Times* suggested that this controversy 'blocked his chances of further ecclesiastical advancement'. Mould-breakers have trouble inside the Church as well as outside it.

A child is not simply 'a chip off the old block'. It inherits genes from both parents, and genetic inheritance is perpetuated over many generations. Fathers and mothers do not create as God creates: they only transmit genetic codes. As a biologist, Richard Dawkins is well aware of these issues. He prefers the 'African Eve' to the dominant male Adam. He does not conceptualize God as an old man with a beard, and his attempt to publish *The Blind Watchmaker* in a version where he referred to God as 'she' throughout suggests a strong sympathy with feminist arguments; but he brushes the problem aside in *The God Delusion,* asking:

> What is the difference between a non-existent male and a non-existent female? . . . I am not attacking any particular version of God or gods. I am attacking God, all gods, anything and everything supernatural, wherever and whenever they have been invented.[13]

He offers no comfort to those who propose changing 'Our Father' to 'Our Mother' or 'Our Parent' because he thinks that the whole debate is pointless.

The Bible as magic

The Genesis stories are perhaps the equivalent in religion of the amoeba in biology: an early stage of development, with much more to come; but for centuries after the Bible was compiled in a written form, it came to be regarded with such awe that a critical analysis of its contents was unthinkable. Even today, many churchgoers suspend their critical judgement during the reading of the Old Testament lesson. It is Holy Writ. It is unassailable. Many, perhaps most, Muslims regard the Qur'an in the same sort of way: it was designed as exhortation, to be declaimed but not to be analysed.

For most of the long history of the Old Testament documents, very few people were able to read, and until the Reformation the Bible was available in Europe only in the dead languages, Hebrew and classical Greek and Latin. Most people had to rely on the parish priest to tell them what was in it. Some of the parish clergy knew little Latin, so they relied on memory, and some very garbled accounts were passed on. The Bible was not a collection of books to be read, but an object of reverence with an almost magical significance.

Every church had a Bible, but until the sixteenth century, it was in Latin, and so large and heavy that it took a strong man even to open it. It was kept locked. The Bible was not there to be read. In some English villages, the practice of weighing a supposed witch against the church Bible survived into the eighteenth century. If the accused outweighed the Bible, that was proof of guilt. The Bible was, and still is, a symbol of absolute truth. Even today, in a court of law or the office of a Commissioner for Oaths, most people swear on the Bible – though there are alternatives in these multicultural times.

What made the Bible accessible to the ordinary Christian? Technology, in the shape of the invention of the printing press. Once it was possible to print and distribute cheap and reliable copies in place of the laboriously copied manuscripts that had kept the monks busy for generations, people clamoured to read for themselves. Johannes Gutenberg set up his press in Germany about 1449, and printed the first complete Bible. William Caxton set up his own press in Westminster in the 1470s. The demand that the Bible should be available in the common tongue became irresistible. By the early sixteenth century, scholars were at work composing fresh translations in place of the Latin versions in the Vulgate, which were mainly the work of St Jerome at the end of the fourth century. The translation of the Bible into the vernacular became one of the principal aims of the Protestant reformers. Luther and other scholars on the Continent by-passed St Jerome and went back to the ancient Hebrew texts. The English scholar William Tyndale[14] went to Germany to learn from them. He translated parts of the Old Testament, including the creation story, from the Hebrew into incomparable English: 'Darkenesse was vpon the depe, and the spirite of God moved vpon the water. Than God sayde, Let there be lyghte, and there was lyghte.'

Tyndale's version was published in Germany in 1526. Translations of the Bible were still forbidden in England, and his was publicly burned; but there was an enormous demand for it. In Henry VIII's time, attempts were made to prevent consignments from reaching England, but even the British Navy and the coastguards were unable to keep them out. Tyndale was executed in the Spanish Netherlands as a heretic, but his translation is still in print today.

Even in the Southern European countries which stayed Catholic, there was a demand for translation,[15] but it was in the newly Protestant countries that the Bible became the central tenet of faith. It retained its magical and symbolic significance, it was still absolute Truth; but it was also a symbol of revolt against the old authority of Rome and kingship. When relatively uneducated people were able to read biblical texts for themselves, they naturally did not always understand what they were reading. The creation story took hold of their imagination: it looked simple, it explained the origin of everything, and it came right at the beginning. Some people have never progressed beyond that level, and it seems at times that Richard Dawkins, despite his scientific scholarship, is one of them.

Interpreting the Old Testament

In the past century and a half, the documents of the Old Testament have been analysed, pored over and tested with all the methods that modern scientific investigation now offers in the process called biblical exegesis. Jewish, Muslim and Christian scholars have of course been working on them for much longer than that – going back to the earliest sources in Hebrew, correcting errors and mistranslations; but archaeologists, palaeontologists, ancient historians, geologists and other specialists have been able to add enormously to our understanding, partly as a result of large-scale excavations. Techniques like carbon dating and computer modelling can now be used to analyse documents and date artefacts. Linguistic analysis helps us to get closer to the original meaning of passages. Fresh translations of the Old Testament draw on all this knowledge, and clarify the original meaning of what was originally a collection of ancient and obscure Hebrew texts.

The texts and the new interpretations have been exhaustively analysed in biblical commentaries. Bible scholars use much the same research methods as physical scientists: they establish facts where they can, they formulate hypotheses and then try to test them out – often by scientific methods. It is very difficult to believe that Richard Dawkins knows nothing of all this work.

Richard Dawkins and Creationism

Creationists hold that the Bible is the literal Word of God, factual in every detail. Richard Dawkins attacks them for their lack of scientific knowledge, but not for their failure to acknowledge other forms of biblical scholarship, since he does not acknowledge it himself.

Most people now recognize that the Old Testament was recorded a very long time ago, in another language, and by people whose own limitations and failings sometimes get in the way of the message; but to Creationists, the Bible is 'the Good Book', the direct Word of God to be quoted freely in English (usually in the Authorised Version of 1611), and applied directly to their own lives. They hold tenaciously to the story of the creation in the book of Genesis. In the United States, there are now several Creation Museums. One in Cincinnatti, Ohio, has been constructed at a cost of $25 million, where young visitors are greeted by a talking model of *Tyrannosaurus Rex*. The dinosaur tells them, 'Of course we lived at the same time as humans. God made dinosaurs on the same day as Adam. And later we drank from the same water as Adam's children.' There is an auditorium where visitors can undergo 'the Creation Experience'. The seats shake, gusts of wind and sprays of water sweep across the seats. Visitors are informed that the book of Genesis is 'the only real history book . . . an eye-witness account written by God himself', and that they should not believe 'what secular astronomers say'. The publicity for this enterprise describes the theory of evolution as 'brainwashing' and blamed it for the rise in teenage suicides. These are said to be caused by the sheer hopelessness of being taught that human beings 'came from slime' and are 'just animals'.[16]

Richard Dawkins is outraged by these ideas, which flatly contradict all his training and experience as a biologist, and deny the theory of evolution. In *The Blind Watchmaker* he writes that Creationists 'actually have an interest in perpetrating falsehoods ... to make statements which encourage others to believe that there never *were* any ancestors is to debauch language and betray truth.'[17] It was when he was writing this passage that he proposed to break off, and go out and dig the garden to get rid of his anger. He never takes part in public debates with Creationists. He pours scorn on their claim that the universe was created only 6,000 years ago. If that was the case, he says, we would not be able to see 'any of the 100,000 million or so other galaxies whose existence modern cosmology acknowledges'.[18]

Today, the campaigning Creationists have shifted ground. They no longer seek an outright confrontation with Darwinism. A complete denial of the theory of evolution is difficult to sustain against all the evidence. What they ask for now is that Creationism and evolution should be taught side by side, so that children can 'make up their own minds'.[19] This appeals to public instincts of fair play. They offer a theory of 'Intelligent Design' which is very different from the Astronomer Royal's 'we were no accident waiting to happen'. Their argument rests on a specific claim: that a minuscule biological organism called the flagellum is inherently complex, and not derived from simpler organisms. Darwin himself said that if ever science discovered an organism which could not have developed by natural selection from a simpler organism, his theory would collapse. Richard Dawkins dismisses the flagellum in four pages of detailed scholarly argument (a longer treatment than he was prepared to give to Thomas Aquinas). Here he is on his own professional ground as a biologist. He states with some authority that the flagellum motor is not irreducibly complex. The falsity of the Creationist case has been massively and embarrassingly documented, and 'Intelligent Design' theory is nonsense.

CHALLENGING RICHARD DAWKINS

Here is the message that an imaginary 'intelligent design theorist' might broadcast to scientists: 'If you don't understand how something works, never mind. Just give up, and say God did it . . . Don't squander precious ignorance by researching it away. We need those glorious gaps as a last refuge for God.'[20]

He notes that the flagellum theory is being actively promoted by Professor Phillip E. Johnson, a lawyer (not a biologist), who founded the Institute of Discovery in Seattle. His comments on Professor Johnson are remarkably restrained. He merely says in a footnote that Phillip E. Johnson founded the Phillip E. Johnson Award for Liberty and Truth in BIOLA, the Bible Institute of Los Angeles, and that the first recipient of the award was Phillip E. Johnson.[21]

Richard Dawkins writes at some length about 'the murky underworld of Creationist propaganda'. In the United States, the Creationist movement now involves multi-million dollar investments in television and publishing houses, and massive coverage on the Internet – all the apparatus of media publicity. Now the movement has spread to Europe. It is of real concern in the British educational system – particularly in some of the new city academies, which have wealthy Creationist backers and are virtually free of local authority control. As Richard Dawkins points out, benefactors can control the ethos of a city academy, influence the appointment of governors and determine policy for the inclusion or exclusion of students.[22] In 2006, the Royal Society found it necessary to issue a statement opposing the teaching of Creationism in schools. This states that Creationism is 'not consistent with the evidence from geology, astronomy and physics that the solar system, including Earth, formed about 4,800 years ago'.[23] but the British Government has left the door open for Creationist teaching. In early 2007, Lord Adonis, the education minister, announced that Creationism may be taught in schools – any schools, not just city academies – as long as it is not taught as Biology. So children may now, apparently, be taught Creationism in Religious Education, and Evolution in Biology, at the discretion of their teachers.

One of the main reasons why Richard Dawkins has set up his atheist charity is because he wants to combat Creationist teaching in schools,[24] but it is doubtful whether the arrival of quantities of atheist pamphlets and DVDs is likely to improve the situation. He is also bent on opposing Roman Catholicism and Islam, and no form of religious teaching, even the milder versions of Quakerism or Unitarianism, gets a kind word from him. We can expect some very muddled children to go home and ask their parents awkward questions.

Creationism in the United States

How can we account for the rise of Creationism in the twenty-first century, when it looked as though the Darwinist analysis of evolution had come to be generally accepted? It is a long story, and one which Richard Dawkins ignores in his contempt for the flagellum theory. He opposes the new Creationism not because it is unhistorical, but because it is unscientific. As so often, the reader needs to pay attention not only to what he says, but to what he does *not* say. The many gaps in his view of biblical scholarship need to be plugged.

Briefly, when the Pilgrim Fathers (Protestant refugees from England and Holland) sailed on the Mayflower in 1620, they took the King James Version of the Bible with them. At that time, it was new and exciting. In the 1600s, there were so many different versions of Bible texts circulating that King James I called a conference of 54 learned clergy at Hampton Court, and commanded them to draw up a definitive version.

Large committees usually produce very poor prose, but this one produced a masterpiece. It relied heavily on Tyndale's work, and many of its phrases now enrich the English language. Richard Dawkins values it 'as literature', and gives a long list of phrases he appreciates.[25] It was published in 1611, and it has remained 'the Authorised Version' to this day.

Some Americans, particularly in the Baptist colleges of the southern states, have continued to insist on the literal interpretation of this version. After decades of heated debate, the US Supreme Court declared Creationist doctrine unconstitutional in 1947. The American Constitution firmly separates church and state, and religious teaching is not allowed in the school system; but the balance of power remains with the individual states, and not with the Federal Government, and that leaves room for litigation. In 2006, there were law suits in some 20 American states, mainly in the south and the north-west of the USA, aimed at the introduction of state law requiring that the Genesis version of Creation be taught as divine revelation.

President Jimmy Carter, in a thoughtful book on the subject, thinks that this return to fundamentalism is a reaction against the resurgence of Islamic fundamentalism in the Middle East. He is a lifelong and committed Baptist himself. He values the Bible, but he does not believe that biblical texts – taken at random, usually taken from the early chapters of the Old Testament, and read in the sixteenth-century King James Version of the Bible, in English – represent the rock-solid unassailable Word of God. He writes:

It seems obvious to me that the Bible presents God's spiritual message, but that the ancient authors of the Holy Scriptures were not experts in geology, biology or cosmology, and were not blessed with the use of electron microscopes, carbon-dating techniques or the Hubble telescope. I've never been bothered by verses in the Bible stating that the earth was flat . . . or that the world was created in six calendar days as we know them.[26]

He describes the new Christian fundamentalists as illiberal, anti-democratic, male-dominant, rigid, narrow-minded and angry – sometimes resorting to 'verbal and even physical abuse against those who interfere with the implementation of their agenda'. Their aim is a return to the values of the book of Genesis. He says that they ignore the principles of social justice, provoke conflict, and rely on fear rather than rational persuasion. He is a former Democratic president, writing about a Republican administration, so his analysis has a political edge, but it is a powerful plea against reactionary influences in the White House and the Pentagon.

Fundamentalism in Roman Catholicism

In his many attacks on Roman Catholicism, Richard Dawkins does not touch on Vatican attitudes to the interpretation of the Bible. Biblical teaching has never been central to Roman Catholic religious observance, which lays greater emphasis on tradition and ritual. Many lay Roman Catholics are familiar only with the Bible passages selected for reading at the Mass. Biblical exegesis was not officially approved by the Vatican until the 1940s. The Jerusalem Bible of 1966 included a commentary which made it plain that the early chapters of the Bible need not be taken literally, noting that they 'visualise the situation of all mankind in the persons of Adam and Eve'. They were not straightforward historical reportage. However, despite the excellent work done by Roman Catholic scholars in the last half century or so, there has always been a strong undertow to literalist interpretation.

In December 2005, the German Government published a

'test of faith' for foreign pilgrims applying for visas to attend Pope Benedict XVI's first papal trip to Germany. According to press reports, 'phoney pilgrims' were to be deterred by such questions as 'Who were the first people?' and 'As a result of the sin committed by Adam and Eve, in what situation do we live?' The 'correct' answers were (a) Adam and Eve, and (b) Original Sin. This literalism may be sufficient to deter Albanian or Kosovan refugees intent on illegal immigration, but it is dismaying to Catholic biblical scholars.

Pope Benedict's first papal Encyclical, *Deus Caritas Est*, develops the same theme. The former Cardinal Ratzinger embarks on a description of 'the biblical account of creation' as literal as that of a fundamentalist from the American Bible belt.[27] It is based, not on the account of the first man and the first woman in Genesis 1, where they are given joint dominion over the earth, but on the second account in Genesis 2. In this version, God creates Adam first. It is only when he realizes that Adam is going to be lonely that he puts him to sleep, takes out one of his ribs, and creates a secondary sort of human, Eve, to keep him company.[28] This is the version of creation depicted by Michaelangelo on the ceiling of the Sistine Chapel. Adam, stretched out in his naked glory, reaches a hand out to God. God reaches down, and the divine spark crackles from the tips of the Almighty's fingers; and where is Eve? She is waiting, veiled and modest, in the shelter of the Almighty's left arm, to be introduced as an afterthought. Probably many pilgrims, craning their necks uncomfortably, never even find her. It is in this chapel, under this image, that the cardinals have met for centuries to elect popes.

Pope Benedict's most recent book, *Jesus of Nazareth* (2007), has been treated with a mixture of praise and criticism by Cardinal Montini of Milan. The cardinal, himself a biblical scholar, described the book as 'beautiful', but not as biblical exegesis. He 'respectfully' raised questions about the Pope's scriptural expertise and his use of critical sources, saying that the Pope 'hardly ever cites the possible variations in biblical texts, and does not discuss the value of the manuscripts'. The book is a personal witness to faith, but the Pope is 'not an exegete'.[29]

Richard Dawkins has launched a powerful attack on the Old Testament on the grounds that God is represented as a cruel and bullying tyrant, and the actions of his chief supporters are morally reprehensible; but this is based on a basic misunderstanding of the ancient mythical accounts which come at the outset. Curiously enough, his two chief targets, the Creationist movement and the Papacy, do exactly the same thing. It is difficult to see how he can follow his blistering attack on the book of Genesis with a blistering attack on those who, like him, take it literally. Three sets of misunderstandings do not add up to a balanced analysis.

Like the Creationist movement and the present Pope, if we may judge from his writing, Dawkins sweeps aside the extensive work of scholars in many fields who have laboured to explain, to analyse and to evaluate these ancient and precious documents. Since he restricts the word 'evolution' to the field of biology, he cannot see that this is another kind of evolution: the evolution of ideas about God and social justice over a period of centuries.

Key points

- Richard Dawkins' anger against 'the God of the Old Testament' is based on a literal reading of the text, and largely based on quotations from the book of Genesis.
- The early Bible stories are pre-history, coming from a pastoral, non-literate society: they are myth, not reportage.
- They reflect the starting-point in the evolution of ideas

about God. The rest of the Old Testament (which Richard Dawkins does not deal with) describes how, through centuries of sin and suffering, the Jewish people came to understand God's purposes and to look for a Messiah.

- The texts have been analysed and interpreted with all the methods available to modern scholars in a variety of fields (biblical exegesis).

- Richard Dawkins opposes the Creationist movement on scientific grounds, but does not deal with its historical origins, its literal interpretation of the Old Testament, or its political and social implications.

- For the past half century, Roman Catholics have accepted biblical exegesis, but some (including the present Pope) have reverted to a literal view of the Old Testament.

- Creationist and Roman Catholic teachings are the main targets of Richard Dawkins' attack in *The God Delusion*, and attacking these teachings will be the main focus of his atheist charity; but it seems that they share more than he is prepard to admit.

5

Down to Earth

Richard Dawkins approves of Jesus Christ. He once wrote an article for a journal named *Free Inquiry* entitled 'Atheists for Jesus', and was given a T-shirt bearing this logo. He says he wore it. He commends Jesus' 'moral superiority' and says that he was 'surely one of the great ethical innovators of history'; but he adds, 'if he existed and whoever wrote his script if he didn't'.[1]

Jesus Christ is not a character in *Dr Who*. He was a real person, with a known history. There is no more reason to doubt his historical existence than to doubt the existence of Socrates (five centuries earlier) or Alexander the Great (four centuries earlier). We have extensive evidence of his life and his ministry in the four Gospels of the New Testament. Richard Dawkins knows about this evidence, but he demands to know, 'Who wrote it, and when? How did they know what to write? Did they, in their time, really mean what we, in our time, understand them to be saying?'

These are good questions. Theologians and historians have been asking them for centuries. Richard Dawkins knows the questions, but seems unacquainted with the answers. The subject is of such importance to Christians that it has been endlessly studied. The texts have been the subject of competing and contradictory dogmatic assertions, fought over, mistranslated, misunderstood, and overlaid with pious assertions and sickly sentimentality for nearly 2,000 years. Perhaps that is enough to put some enquirers off; but the original evidence must be treated on its merits, and studied by the methods of rational enquiry. It cannot be dismissed so lightly.

The evidence

Richard Dawkins asserts that 'Nobody knows who the four evangelists were, but they certainly never met Jesus personally.'[2] This is simply untrue. The internal evidence of the Gospels is that Matthew, Luke and John knew Jesus well, travelled with him, talked with him, and were his disciples throughout his ministry. Mark, younger than Matthew or Luke, may not have met Jesus personally, but we know that he accompanied Paul on his missionary journeys (where he is called John Mark), and Luke wrote the account of those journeys in the Acts of the Apostles. The Acts ends with a reference to Paul's stay in Rome under house arrest. Paul, like Peter, died in the persecutions of Nero, who was emperor from 54 to 68, probably in the year 64 or 65. Nobody doubts the historical existence of Nero.

The Gospels of Matthew, Mark and Luke are known as the Synoptic Gospels. 'Synoptic' means 'with the same eye': that is, they are based on reportage from eye-witnesses of the same events and written in the same period. The Fourth Gospel, that of John, was written later. John was a young man when he met Jesus, and the Gospel dates from about the year 90, by which time he would probably have been in his eighties.[3]

These documents are of very different quality from the tribal myths of the early part of the Old Testament. By the first century of the Christian era, written records were common. The evangelists were reporting the same story, though from somewhat different angles. Richard Dawkins alleges that there are 'glaring contradictions' between their accounts.[4] There are certainly some differences, but we should expect differences. If we hear three witnesses in a court of law testifying to the same events, and they all tell exactly the same story, word for word, we begin to suspect collusion. If we read precisely the same account of a political crisis or a royal visit in the *Telegraph*, *Guardian* and *Sun*, we might conclude that two of the three reporters were falling down on the job. Matthew, Mark and Luke were distinct characters, with personalities and interests of their own, and each had his own story to tell.

Mark probably wrote his Gospel in Rome. Internal evidence dates it to about AD 65, and those of Matthew and Luke to between the years 70 and 80. Parchment and papyrus wear out, so we no longer have the originals, but the earliest documents we have today were transcribed only about 35 years after the crucifixion – that can be verified by carbon dating. There is a Greek version of Mark's Gospel in the British Library in London that dates from about the year 90 – only 60 years after the crucifixion. Visitors can look at it, though they may not touch it. It is displayed open, so that those able to read Greek may check the text.

Mark's Gospel was evidently written first, because both Matthew and Luke quote from him. We know that there were other, earlier manuscripts which have been lost through the centuries: a previous version of Matthew's Gospel in Hebrew, said to be 'strongly Aramaic', which was known in the Middle Ages; and a document known to scholars as 'Q' on which Luke and Matthew both drew, as well as quoting Mark. 'Q' stands for *Quelle*, which is German for 'source'. That is also lost. Even so, the documents we can handle and read are as close to the actual life of Jesus as something written today would be of events in the 1960s or 1970s. These accounts were written by people who knew Jesus.

The internal evidence of the Synoptic Gospels tells us a good deal about the personalities of their authors. They were educated men. Matthew was a tax collector, Mark was Paul's young missionary colleague, Luke was a doctor. They write quite simply of what they know – in fairly basic Greek, without literary flourishes.

Are they reliable witnesses? They are much more reliable than many of the 'lost' gospels that are currently being republished and explored on television; but it will be simpler to follow the main story first, and deal with the variants later. We are talking about fact, not fiction; the four evangelists were not concerned to set people puzzles and cryptograms like those in *The Da Vinci Code*. They had a remarkable story to tell, and because they were different kinds of men, they told it differently.

Richard Dawkins on 'the fatherless man'

To many millions of Christians in five continents, the story of the life of Jesus Christ is the story of how God himself came down to earth to show human beings how to live. Jesus is the promised Messiah, the Saviour. Richard Dawkins chooses to refer to him as 'the fatherless man'. There is a long passage in *The God Delusion* in which he caricatures what he calls 'the beliefs of a mainstream Christian'.[5] Christians are represented as holding that:

1 the mother of 'the fatherless man' was a virgin;
2 he raised a friend from the dead;
3 he came alive after dying himself;
4 he 'disappeared bodily into the sky';
5 he listens to you if you 'murmur your thoughts privately to yourself';
6 he sees everything, even if nobody else does;
7 his virgin mother went to heaven without dying first;

8 bread and wine turn into his body and blood if blessed by a priest.

These are the doctrines known to Christians as the Virgin Birth, the raising of Lazarus, the Resurrection, the Ascension, prayer, omniscience, the Assumption of the Blessed Virgin Mary and Transubstantiation. The last two are specifically Roman Catholic doctrines. Roman Catholics are required by papal decree to believe that the Virgin Mary was directly translated to heaven, and that the bread and wine in the Eucharist is literally Christ's body and blood. Other Christians are not, and many Roman Catholics find these doctrines difficult.

Nearly all Christians will readily admit they do not know the whole story of the birth of Jesus, the precise details of what happened to Lazarus, or the exact logistics of the ascension. The essential items of Christian faith in this list are the third, the fifth and the sixth: that Jesus Christ rose from the dead, that he listens to prayer, and that he is united with God the Creator. Not only is Richard Dawkins' list a travesty of 'what Christians believe': it omits nearly all the facts and all the evidence. So what do Christians believe? Behind all the theological complexities and the debates are some fairly straightforward propositions which can be rationally supported.

A Christian rationale

The universe and everything in it cannot simply be the result of a cosmic accident, because we have evidence at every turn of design, and we are constantly coming across unexpected patterns of order in what was previously thought to be sheer muddle (chaos). The Creator cannot be an impersonal force, like electricity, because impersonal forces cannot create personalities. Human personality is the most precious thing we know, so we think of him in personal terms. The Creator is *at least* a person, but not simply a person, like Bill Bryson or Albert Einstein: more than a person; supra-personal.

The evidence of science suggests – but can neither prove nor disprove – that our Creator is supremely powerful and supremely intelligent. Thomas Aquinas described him as the superlative: he said that is what the term 'God' means. God is the author of the highest things we know – Truth, Beauty, Justice. He is the ultimate Law-giver. Laws – including the natural laws so often cited by scientists – do not make themselves, any more than universes do. We cannot contemplate our Creator without coming up against the limits of time and space as we experience them.

Religious fundamentalism has been a channel for a new demand for 'proof' – here-and-now proof, absolute proof, of the Creator's existence and involvement in our world. God is capable of miracles; but he may not perform them on demand – or as often as some people would like to believe. However, Christians believe that he intervened in human history just once, to give us an example of how to live.

For God to enter his own creation was a remarkable thing to do, and we must make the best sense of it we can. Suppose if you can, just for a moment, that you are God. The world you made is in chaos and confusion. You cannot continually intervene to sort it out, because you have given human beings free will, and they must learn to live with the consequences of their actions. You could take free will away from them, and turn them into zombies, but you will not do that, because free will, the capacity to choose between different courses of action, is what makes them human. They are abusing it, and making the wrong decisions; but you cannot be constantly interfering, threatening here, bribing there, as the old Greek gods were thought to do. Free will must be respected. The only thing you can do is to go down yourself, become human like them, and teach them from inside their system: not with thunderbolts and earthquakes, but with calm reason and example.

You choose your time and place: the time has to be when the human race has advanced sufficiently to be ready to listen to your message, and the place has to be one where it can be heard. So you train the Jews – a difficult people of warring nomads – over the centuries. It is not easy, but they do listen. They develop a religion with higher moral standards and a greater sense of personal devotion than the neighbouring tribes, and are taught to await a Messiah. Their land is at the juncture of the three continents known in their day – Europe, Africa and Asia. It is occupied by the imperial forces of Rome – but in time the widespread Roman jurisdiction, Roman roads and Roman culture will become the means of transmitting the message.

Christians were perfectly clear from the earliest times that there is one God. Jesus Christ is not an appendage to God, but the revelation of the one God in the history of our world: rather like a company chairman going and working on the shop floor and getting his hands dirty. That may be closer to modern understanding than the idea of Christ 'coming down from heaven'.

Given that God would not take away our free will, this was surely the only way to reach us. Even the Almighty cannot do what is contradictory. If he sets up laws for running the universe, he cannot keep breaking them himself. So God came into his creation as a character in the drama – a template of how human beings should live, and how they can achieve peace and brotherhood. In order to do this, God had to be human: born of a woman, like everyone else, intervening in our muddles and confusions, to set us back on the right track. If that sounds unlikely, all the scientific discussion about spinning worlds and disappearing bosons and double helixes sounds unlikely, too; but it is really happening, right now. This is what physical scientists call a Singularity. The evidence for the life of Jesus Christ is at least as sound as the evidence for the Big Bang. Because we are finite creatures, we cannot know everything about it, but what we do know takes us a good deal further than Richard Dawkins is trying to suggest.

The birth of Jesus Christ

How does the story begin? Matthew, Mark and Luke all start at different points. Mark begins when Jesus is already an adult, and tells the story of how he went to John the Baptist to be baptized before commencing his ministry. Matthew, the closest to Judaic tradition, is concerned with the family tree. He begins by reciting Joseph's descent from David – a typical Old Testament account of a male line of descent, despite the fact that the main point of the story is that Joseph was not Jesus' biological father. As Richard Dawkins points out, this is irrelevant. A biologist would naturally seize on this point; but Matthew's mind runs on orthodox Jewish tramlines, and he is concerned that this marvellous birth shall be demonstrated to be the fulfilment of Old Testament prophecy:

> For a child has been born for us, a son given to us; authority rests upon his shoulders; and he is named Wonderful Counsellor, Mighty God, Everlasting Father, Prince of Peace. His authority shall grow continually, and there shall be endless peace for the throne of David and his kingdom. He will establish it and uphold it with justice and righteousness from this time forward, and for evermore.[6]

Luke is the only source for most of the stories of the nativity which are celebrated in churches every Christmas. His first chapter tells the stories of the angel's annunciation to Mary, Mary's song of acceptance, her visit to her cousin Elizabeth and the birth of John the Baptist. Perhaps because Luke was a doctor, he seems to be more sympathetic than the other writers to the concerns of women, and professionally interested in matters of conception and birth. Some people think that Luke heard these stories from Mary the mother of Jesus herself. They may have a factual base, they may be legend, incorporated into the narrative by early scribes; but they do not affect the account given of Jesus' ministry during the period when Luke knew him and worked with him.

Richard Dawkins says: 'Jesus was one of many charismatic figures who emerged in Palestine around his time.'[7] *Charisma* is a much-abused word. The original Greek meaning is one touched by divinity, or by the power of God. The examples Richard Dawkins gives are Haile Selassie, Elvis Presley and Princess Diana, so he seems to be using the word simply in the modern sense of 'a celebrity'. Even so, it is an odd choice of examples. There were certainly other people in the Middle East at the time who claimed divine inspiration. Jesus warned his disciples against false prophets; and told them that the test was always in what they did, not in what they said. He asked 'Are grapes gathered from thorns, or figs from thistles? In the same way, every good tree bears good fruit, but the bad tree bears bad fruit.'[8] He was living in a fruit-growing area, and his friends would have seen the point of that illustration. Grapes, figs and other fruit still reach our supermarkets from Israel in the winter.

Richard Dawkins finds the Christian claim that Jesus was born of a virgin entirely unbelievable. A biologist would. Biologists take it for granted that all mammals have two parents, one male and one female. We are not told exactly how Mary came to be bearing a child. To many Christians, it seems impertinent to ask; but in the ancient world, the idea that the world would be saved by one born of God (or a god) and a human mother was very familiar. The mother would have to be a virgin, because that was the only way in which the divine fatherhood could be determined. There were many myths and stories of a virgin birth circulating round the Middle East. Religious thinkers in a number of different cultures had worked it out for themselves that the only way in which God could put the world right was by divine intervention. Just how this ancient dream became reality in terms of the creation of a special human genome is beyond our understanding; but if the entire universe has an Intelligent Designer, this process, achieved through centuries of inheritance, could be part of the design.

Jesus was born in Bethlehem, despite Richard Dawkins' rather muddled attempts to suggest that he was born in Nazareth. In the intervals when there is peace between the Israelis and the Palestinians, it is still possible to visit the place where tradition says that the birth took place. This may not be certain, but it is much more than a claim made by the local tourist guides. A Greek philosopher called Justin Martyr visited the site about the year 135.[9] He recorded in his *Dialogue with Trypho* that it was already a holy place, much venerated by Christians. He says that pilgrims had started visiting the site soon after the resurrection. The Emperor Hadrian had tried to discourage them by building a Roman temple there, but that simply identified the place more clearly, and made it easier for the Christians to find.

The site is not the sort of thatched stable beloved of Botticelli and reproduced on Christmas cards, but something more permanent – a cave, a hole in the rock. In that part of Palestine, the local people still shelter their animals in caves. It lies beneath the Church of the Nativity, down a narrow flight of steps made slippery by the feet of countless pilgrims through the centuries, underneath the high altar. It is a very ancient place, small and dark, lit only by oil lamps, and the walls are blackened with the lamp grease of centuries.

Mary was probably very young when she bore her child, and was probably a virgin. Good Jewish girls were often married at puberty. Was she a perfect human being? The Roman Catholic doctrine of the Immaculate Conception holds that Mary was incapable of sin; but it was not officially promulgated until 1854.[10] Other Christians think that this doctrine owes more to piety than to sound theology. If Mary had been incapable of sin, she would not have been fully human, and her child would not have been human, either. Mary had to possess free will, and to be able to make a choice. If she did not have the power to make a choice, her submission to the divine will would have been meaningless. She was offered a stupendous task. She could have refused; but she was young and devout, and she accepted it, with all the social shame and the pain and the sorrow it was to bring her.

Most medieval paintings of the annunciation show the mother of Jesus uplifted, glorified and triumphant in the spirit of the Magnificat – 'My soul magnifies the Lord, and my spirit rejoices in God my saviour: for he has looked with favour on the lowliness of his servant'; but a painting by Lorenzo Lotto gives a very different interpretation. Mary is aghast and frightened at the burden that is laid upon her; and the family cat, standing next to her, has all its hair on end as it confronts the invading angel. But Mary said, 'Let it be with me according to your word.' Her acceptance of God's will was complete.

Was he the Son of God?

There is no evidence that Jesus ever called himself 'the Son of God'. Other people gave him that title, but all the evidence we have from the New Testament is that he called himself 'the

Son of Man'. He spoke Aramaic, and in that language 'the Son of Man' was a common phrase, a polite way of saying 'I', that applied to everybody. It was not a special title.

When people asked him if he was the Messiah, he usually passed the question back to them with some comment like 'Do you think so?' or 'You say so'. He asked the disciples who they thought he was, and according to Matthew, it was Peter who answered, 'You are the Messiah, the Son of the Living God.'[11] That was an answer from the patriarchal Jewish culture; but if we do not think in Old Testament terms of 'the Father', we do not need the concept of 'the Son'. The full Christian doctrine is that Jesus Christ *is* God: the God who made heaven and earth.

Christians have traditionally called Jesus 'the Son', but this is an allegory, not to be taken literally. The relationship between a father and a son was the closest relationship Jewish social and religious experience could express. Without a modern knowledge of genetics, they really did think that a son was an exact copy of his father in both appearance and character – 'Like father, like son'; but no one was claiming that Jesus Christ was the product of a sexual union between God the Creator and the girl Mary. In the Greek myths, the gods were said to have come down from Olympus and had sexual intercourse with women, but the Jews were strict monotheists. Their reverence for Jehovah would have precluded such fantasies. Human beings know only one natural means of 'begetting', and this clearly was never intended.

Jesus called God *Abba,* Father, because he grew up in a Jewish culture, and had a good Jewish education. He told his disciples that God was everyone's father. Talk to God, he said, as if you were talking to your own father, intimately, but with respect: Our Father, *Nôtre Père, Pater Noster.*[12] The disciples would have understood this, because they all came from the same culture.

The older form of the Christian creed refers to Jesus 'sitting on the right hand of God'. The modern version is 'sitting *at* the right hand of God'. Some medieval painters took the older phrase quite literally, depicting a massive Father with his right hand extended, and a tiny Christ sitting on the palm. The reference comes from Mark's Gospel.[13] At a banquet, the guest of honour sits on the right-hand side of the host, and Mark surely meant only that 'the Son' occupied a special place of honour in his 'Father's' household.

Perhaps Christians ought to abandon the old Jewish tradition of talking about 'the Father' and 'the Son', but that would be very difficult. 'Our Father' is Jesus Christ's own phrase, given by him to his disciples. It has been reproduced in priceless manuscripts, carved in marble, inscribed in miniature on threepenny bits. There was a time when every child knew it – though that may not now be the case. It is deeply embedded in our faith. We cannot ignore the analogy, but it is time we made sense of it. If we ignore the issue, we get involved with Muslims who do not understand how God could have a son unless he slept with a woman, and we get tangled in Richard Dawkins' nonsense about 'the fatherless man's father – who is also himself'.[14] 'God the Father' is the Creator. 'God the Son' is God in action in our world.

Christians believe that God himself experienced all the pains and passions of human life, and gave human beings a route back to sanity and peace. Orthodox Jews are still waiting for the Messiah to come. Muslims believe that Jesus was a prophet, but only one of a line of prophets, and that Muhammad had a greater revelation. Many people in the West believe that Jesus was 'just a good man'. Some think that the whole story is a myth. Richard Dawkins appears to think that it is a television script.

Did Jesus know everything?

How could Jesus be God, and at the same time a real human being?

That problem has given the theologians many headaches over the centuries. God is all-powerful and all-knowing, human beings are not. They make mistakes, and they have to learn. There is evidence in the New Testament that Jesus had to learn. He had to learn to walk and talk like other children. He had to learn the Judaic tradition. Luke tells us that when he was about 12, Mary and Joseph took him up to the Temple in Jerusalem, and lost him on the way back. Like any parents, they were panic-stricken, and they went back to find him in the Temple, where he was listening to the teachers, and asking them questions.[15]

In the Gospel narratives, there are at least two instances of occasions where he seems to have changed his mind during his ministry. John tells us that at the wedding feast at Cana,[16] his mother asked him to help their host when the wine ran out, and his first reaction was to refuse. 'Woman, what concern is that to you and me?' Richard Dawkins accuses him of 'dodgy family values' in being rude to his mother;[17] but Jesus was speaking in the local tongue, Aramaic, and 'Woman' was a normal form of address in that language.

The incident is a very revealing one. The basic story – the village wedding, the host's embarrassment, is entirely believable, and so is Mary's reaction. She knows that her son has more than usual powers, and she asks him to help. He hesitates, and tries to evade the issue. It is not yet time for his mission, he wants to keep a low profile; but he responds to his mother's request. Does he turn water into wine? All we are told is that the guests are pleased with what they have to drink, the host's face is saved, and the celebrations continue.

There is another key incident when the Canaanite woman

asks him to help her sick daughter.[18] His first reaction is to say that he has been sent only to help the children of Israel, but when she answers that even the dogs lick up the crumbs that fall from the master's table, he realizes that she is right to ask: his mission is much wider than a Jewish education had led him to believe, and he accepts what she says with much grace. Richard Dawkins alleges that 'Love thy neighbour' only meant 'Love another Jew'.[19] This is evidence that it did not.

The doctrine of *kenosis*[20] is that during his earthly life, God had to restrict himself to the knowledge and understanding of the time in which he had chosen to live. The doctrine has been much debated, but most theologians accept that there had to be some restriction imposed by his humanity. The appearance in any society of a person who knew everything, past, present and future, who could do anything and could be in more than one place at once would have spoiled the whole exercise. He had to enter space and time, and be subject to their limitations. His wisdom was that of God himself, but his knowledge was that of a first-century Jew. He had to learn, because human beings do learn.

What sort of person was he?

We have no information on what Jesus Christ looked like. He must have been of a particular weight and height as an adult, and have had a particular colouring. Was he dark or fair? Not all Israelis are dark. Was his hair curly or straight? Did he wear a beard or go clean-shaven? Artists have drawn and painted him in many different guises, but we really do not know. He is a universal figure for the whole human race. In Britain, he is often portrayed as an Anglo-Saxon; in Italy, as an Italian; Africans see him as black, and Chinese and Japanese as one of their own kind.

According to the Gospels, he was a very unusual young man. He was remarkably free from social prejudice, talking easily and directly to rich and poor alike. He accepted hospitality, but did not pile up funds – indeed, he advised his disciples to travel light, saying that they did not need to carry money or baggage: Matthew, Mark and Luke all report such sayings.[21] He made no effort to cultivate the right people, and was no respecter of persons where matters of principle were involved. He was furiously angry with the money-changers, whose commercial activities defiled the Temple in Jerusalem, but he seems in general to have taken people as he found them. He was equally at home with wealthy men who came to him for spiritual advice, with publicans – tax collectors like Matthew, who worked for the hated Romans – and with despised people like beggars and so-called madmen. He healed lepers, in a society where most people were afraid of contagion, avoiding contact with them at all costs. When he found a group of men about to stone a woman taken in adultery, he pointed out that men had a responsibility for sexual misbehaviour as well as women, and when he asked them which of them was fit to cast the first stone, they fell silent and went away.[22] His disciples were astonished that he talked to the woman, but he talked as freely to women as to men. He was unpretentious and never pompous, a good storyteller, and sometimes he made people laugh.

He was well versed in the Jewish Scriptures, so he could certainly read Hebrew, though the few words of his recorded speech are in Aramaic. He probably spoke some Greek – Matthew, Mark, Luke and John all did, though it was of a fairly rough and ready sort.

When he was prepared to start his mission, he made a retreat, going alone into the bare rocky lands known as 'the wilderness' to work out what he had to do. Matthew, Mark and Luke all tell the story.[23] There, in biblical terms, he was tempted by the devil – or as we might say, he faced his own demons. He knew what he had to do. he did not want to rule the world, or to take part in an insurrection against the Romans. He did not want to court publicity by being saved from death by swooping angels; he refused to turn stones into bread to gain popularity from the hungry masses; he had no desire to rule the kingdoms of the world. He just wanted to teach quietly and peaceably, to reach the individual heart. Thereafter, he simply spoke of his mission as a fact. He taught his disciples how they should live, forecast his own death, and spoke with absolute confidence about the life to come, in which the wrongs and miseries of earthly existence would be put right.

His ethical teaching was simple and clear. Even Richard Dawkins acknowledges that. He replaced the ten prohibitions of the Commandments ('Thou shalt not . . .') with two positive commands: love God, and love your neighbour as much as you love yourself: if you do that, the rest will follow.[24] When a lawyer asked him who his neighbour was, he told him the story of the Good Samaritan:[25] a priest and a Levite ignored the man who had been set upon by thieves, but a Samaritan rescued him. The Samaritans were a despised and alien people in Judaea, so this was rather like telling a story to a member of the British National Party and ending 'and he was a Pakistani'.

He was a good teacher. Like all good teachers, he used examples to illustrate his meaning, and he picked them from the world around him – the corn growing in the fields, the shepherd rounding up his sheep, the house that collapsed because it was built on sand: the sort of thing local people would know about from their own experience.

Did he perform miracles? Many events that have been accounted miracles in the past have been shown to be capable of rational explanation as medical knowledge advances; but

CHALLENGING RICHARD DAWKINS

faithful people, sometimes with the best of intentions, have obscured the field by claiming all sorts of impossible marvels. These have inspired piety in thousands of people through the centuries, but piety is not worth much if it is based on a lie, a misunderstanding, or at best a piece of sentimental wishful thinking. He could have walked on the water and stilled the storm on Lake Galilee[26] – but would he have done so? Greek mythology included stories about gods who controlled the wind and the waves and other aspects of the weather. Is this something the disciples expected him to be able to do, and so perhaps exaggerated a natural event?

It is possible that the miracle stories, like the nativity stories, were inserted into the narratives later by scribes, to emphasize Christ's unique qualities. If he refused the temptation to turn stones into bread to feed the hungry, would he have performed what look like a magician's tricks? Perhaps incidents that have been interpreted as miracles have rational explanations that we are not yet ready to understand. The only honest reaction seems to be to keep an open mind.

Why was he killed?

Jesus antagonized the currency traders in the Temple in Jerusalem by turning their tables over and driving them out.[27] He spoke out against the Pharisees, who were the most strict religious group, calling them hypocrites and blind fools and vipers and whitewashed tombs, clean on the outside, and full of filth, an absolute torrent of invective.[28] Aramaic is a very blunt language. He was accused of saying that he would destroy the Temple.[29] He had a strong following among the poor, who turned out in crowds to welcome him when he entered Jerusalem on a donkey.[30] In other words, he was a trouble-maker, anti-Establishment, with no respect for the people in power. And he was suspected (wrongly) of being part of the Zionist movement, a political group opposed to Roman rule. Reason enough.

He must have known that he was heading for trouble. On the night before he died, he called his disciples together, and told them that one of them would betray him; and that he would suffer and be killed. It was the time of the Jewish Passover, the feast that commemorated the saving of the children of Israel in the time of Moses. He took bread and wine at the supper table, and said, 'This is my body which is broken for you', and, 'This is my blood which is shed for you', and told them to keep a new feast in his memory.[31] This is the origin of what is called the Mass, Holy Communion, the Eucharist or the Last Supper. Christians differ over exactly what he meant: some think that every time it is celebrated, the bread and wine become literally his body and blood; some think that it is simply a memorial; and some are content simply to do what they were told to do, and to leave the meaning to God.

The disciples did not understand what was going on. They were sad and confused. He led them out of Jerusalem, across the valley into the Garden of Gethsemane, and told them to keep watch for him, but they all fell asleep. They must have been exhausted. He was left alone among the olive trees, to fight his own battle. He was God, but he was also a human being, and he must have known only too well what lay ahead of him if he stood his ground. From the darkness of the garden, he could look across to the lights of the city: the Temple, the High Priest's house, the palace, the prison. He must have known what that prison was like – the beatings, the screams, the smells, the pain, the total subjection to mindless brutality.

He could have walked away. Every human instinct in him must have told him to walk away. He was still quite young, he was healthy, he was doing good work. There was a way out.

Every nerve must have screamed 'Go while there's still time'. He had friends and supporters in Galilee. He prayed to the Creator God he called his Father, 'Let this cup pass from me.' He said 'The spirit is willing, but the flesh is weak' – a clear expression of his dual nature.[32] The God in him knew that he had to suffer and die a slow death. The human being in him was scared. If you stand in Gethsemane (now a collection of gnarled old trees surrounded by railings to stop visitors from stripping them, rather like a small public park), you can imagine that last night of anguish before the soldiers dragged him down the hill and up the other side of the valley by a worn flight of steps to the prison, to be flogged and mocked and sentenced to death.

Judas betrayed him for 30 pieces of silver, and then, overcome with the knowledge of what he had done, killed himself.[33] From the house of the High Priest in Jerusalem, it is possible to see what is called 'The Potter's field' where he is reputed to have committed suicide. Though the land must by now be very valuable, no one has ever built on it. Richard Dawkins is attracted to recent attempts to argue that God sacrificed Judas to achieve the crucifixion.[34] It seems much more likely that Judas was a disappointed Zionist, who thought that Jesus would lead a revolt, or that he just wanted the money, or that he was currying favour with the Temple authorities. Judas, like everyone else, had free will; but if he had not been the agent of betrayal, someone else would have done the same before long. The situation of the just man and the unjust society has all the inevitability of a Greek tragedy.

It is a matter of history that Jesus Christ was crucified when Pontius Pilate was the Roman consul in Jerusalem. Crucifixion was a very slow and painful and public method of execution which the Romans used for conquered people. It was very common. Sometimes the roads around Jerusalem were lined with crosses, and a man dying on every one of them. Roman citizens were despatched more mercifully – with a quick sword blow across the throat. The only reference Richard Dawkins makes to the execution of Jesus is in the form of a particularly tasteless joke from Lenny Bruce.[35]

The four Gospels all describe Jesus' dying in detail. After a long period of acute suffering, he cried *Eloi, eloi, lama sabachthani*, or in modern versions, *Eli, Eli, lema sabachthani*: 'My God, my God, why hast thou forsaken me?'[36] Even in the extremity of pain and exhaustion, he was quoting the Scriptures: the words come from Psalm 22, which, after terrible passages of suffering and despair, ends in praise and trust in God. He was not denying the existence of God, but he had temporarily lost touch with transcendence. Perhaps this was the final earthly experience for God himself – what mystics have described as the 'Dark Night of the Soul'? But for all the suffering, he remembered his task, and his final words were 'It is finished'.

He was buried on the site of the present Church of the Holy Sepulchre. As with the place of his birth, the Romans had tried to deter pilgrims by erecting a temple at the place, but that only made it easier to identify.

The fourth-century historians Socrates and Sozomen tell us that Helena, mother of the Emperor Constantine, made a visit in 327, and ordered a church to be built there.[37] Some people are confused by the fact that the Church of the Holy Sepulchre lies inside the walls of Jerusalem, not 'without (i.e. outside) a city wall', as the hymn 'There is a green hill' says.[38] But Mrs Alexander, who wrote the hymn, was a scholar. She knew that the present site was outside the city wall at the time of the crucifixion. Helena had the walls extended 300 years later to include it.

It is a dark little place, smoky with candles, and of course the tomb is empty. It is not very impressive. When General Gordon of Khartoum visited it in the late nineteenth century, he disliked it so much that he thought it could not possibly be the right place. Some distance away, he found some first century tombs by a rock in the shape of a skull which he thought must be Golgotha. The tomb he thought was the right one lies in a quiet and peaceful garden where it was possible to imagine that first Easter morning. Gordon started a society to restore the garden, and today, trees and wild cyclamen and anemones and other flowers make it a place of devotion. Of course, given wind and natural erosion, the rock may not have looked like a skull 2,000 years ago; but the site is much more evocative of the place of the resurrection than the smoky little tomb in the Church of the Holy Sepulchre. The Jerusalem City Council has built a bus station next door to it, but even the noise and the petrol fumes do not destroy its tranquillity.

Did he rise from the dead?

Richard Dawkins flatly disbelieves in the resurrection on the grounds that when biological organisms die, they stay dead. As we have seen, he does not think that there is an insurmountable difference between life forms and inanimate objects apart from what he calls 'power',[39] but as an atheist, he ignores the possibility that on this one occasion, testified to by hundreds of witnesses, it really happened.

If he finds the resurrection difficult to believe, so did the disciples. It was totally unexpected. Though Jesus had talked about being with them to the end of the world, it seems that they were completely disorganized and dejected after he died. John, who was near the tomb at the time, gives the fullest account.[40] Mary Magdalene saw him first, but did not recognize him immediately in the dim early morning light. She thought that he was the cemetery gardener until he spoke to her. Then she recognized him, and said *Rabboni*, teacher. When she told Peter and John, they ran to the tomb to look for themselves. Young John could run faster. He got there first, but out of respect for the older disciple, he waited, and allowed Peter to enter first. There were no thunderbolts, no lightning flashes, no bursts of heavenly radiance. The young men in white clothes who are said to have reassured the women, and the angel who rolled away the stone and sat on it, sound rather like later embellishments; but the story of a young man speaking quietly to his friends in a garden is compelling.

When Jesus subsequently met his friends, all the accounts say that he had a real body. Doubting Thomas was told to put his hand in his side and feel the wounds.[41] Jesus' mother and members of his family and the disciples all talked to him. As always, he was very matter of fact, and gave himself no airs. Once when the fishermen came ashore from Lake Galilee, he was there on the beach, companionably tending a fire and cooking fish for their breakfast.[42] After that, he appeared to many other people – including the 500 mentioned by Paul in his letter to the Corinthians.[43] He also appeared to people who did not recognize him at the time, walking with them along the road to Emmaus and teaching them.[44] He was teaching all the time. He told them that he must leave them, but 'when the Spirit of Truth comes, he will guide you into all truth'.[45]

He had completed what he had to do on earth. He had taught human beings how to live, how to get on with each other, how to suffer, how to stand up for what they believed in. He could not stay on earth, lead a normal human life, grow old and die as the rest of us do. After a time of teaching his disciples about the coming of the Holy Spirit, and telling them to proclaim the good news to all nations, he went away from them. His message was for all ages, not only for one generation.

As to Richard Dawkins' statement that he 'disappeared

bodily into the sky', all the Gospels tell us is that he disappeared. He assured his closest disciples that they would receive power, and 'a cloud received him out of their sight'.[46] No fuss, no drama. Perhaps the disciples thought that he had gone straight up into the sky. They can have had no idea of what immense distances lay beyond the earth's atmosphere, or of the complexities of the space–time continuum. All they knew was that their Lord had disappeared out of their world. Then two 'men in white apparel' said briskly, 'Ye men of Galilee, why stand ye gazing up into heaven?' So they took the hint, and went back to Jerusalem, to await the Holy Spirit.[47]

For centuries, people have looked for physical traces of the earthly life of Jesus – the Holy Grail, thought to be the cup he drank from at the Last Supper, or the cup in which his blood was caught during the crucifixion (or both); the robe his mother was wearing when he was born; the shroud that covered him in the tomb; the cross on which he was crucified. When supposed relics have been subjected to carbon dating, they have been found to come from a much later period (principally from the time of the Crusades). The Christian faith does not depend on the authenticity of relics. What Jesus Christ left us was a way of living. Material objects so easily become a focus for superstition.

John's interpretation

By any reckoning, the story of Jesus is a remarkable story. Matthew, Mark and Luke give a very plain, factual account, with no sign of special pleading, hidden agendas and prejudice. There is no sign that they are anything but what they say they are: plain men, not scholars, not theologians. They have no axe to grind. They gain no profit from telling their story. Quite often they cannot fully understand what they have seen and heard. They just write it down. They do not seek publicity in the worldly sense. They simply describe what happened – not with drama and literary flourishes, but almost laconically. This is the stuff of reality, not of fiction.

The Fourth Gospel is also the stuff of reality, but it was written some years after the others, after decades of study and contemplation. The author refers to himself as 'the disciple whom Jesus loved', and is generally thought to be St John, known as the Evangelist. A final note in the Gospel says, 'This is the disciple who is testifying to these things, and has written them, and we know that his testimony is true.'[48] The 'beloved disciple' may only have been 20 or 25 when he knew Jesus, and the Fourth Gospel, written some 60 or more years later, reads as though it is based on the reflections of a very old man. He knows what Matthew, Mark and Luke have written, and sometimes draws on their accounts for detail. He probably had a scribe, who may also have been called John. The manuscript bears the marks of editorial work, and possibly the addition of some substantive passages, by another hand. It may have been published by John's disciples after his death. He was the only one of the four Gospel-writers who lived to old age and died a natural death: Matthew, Mark and Luke are all thought to have been martyred;[49] but John has a new perspective – partly because he lived so long and had so much time to think, and partly because he lived in a Greek culture, in what is now Asia Minor, and was able to unite Jewish understanding of the life of Jesus with the classical Greek doctrine of the Logos or Word, the action of the divine principle in the world of men and women. In what is called the Prologue to St John's Gospel, he explains what he believes to be the true meaning of Jesus Christ's life on earth:

In the beginning was the Word, and the Word was with God and the Word was God. He was in the beginning with

God. All things came into being through him, and without him not one thing came into being.[50]

In him was life, 'and the life was the light of all people'. And the light continued to shine in the darkness, and the darkness could not overcome it. 'And the Word became flesh and lived among us, and we have seen his glory, as of a father's only son, full of grace and truth.' This is a Greek scholar's exposition, built on the old apostle's faith, but raising it to a new level of understanding in a predominantly Greek world.

Today, we know enough about the universe to realize that we live in earthly time, set by the solar system, but that our Creator is beyond earthly time. The Prologue to St John's Gospel tells us, 'He was in the world, and the world came into being through him, yet the world did not know him. He came to what was his own.' The experience of what it was like to suffer as a human being was part of God's nature from the time of the creation. Jesus Christ is God the Creator revealed to his creatures in a form they can understand. The Prologue is the traditional gospel for Christmas Day, the one day in the year above all others when we should think about the mysteries of the incarnation – God made flesh. It is the supreme account of how, nearly 2,000 years ago in earthly time, an eternal strand in the mind of our Creator was made manifest.

Key points

- Jesus Christ is an historical figure. The events of his life are fully recorded in the four Gospels which can be dated back to the first century, and which have been preserved and extensively studied.
- Richard Dawkins' outline of what Christians believe about 'the fatherless man' is a deliberate distortion.

- If the universe has an Intelligent Designer, the life of Jesus is a logical part of the design: a way of giving human beings free will, and then showing them how to use it.
- The Jewish formulation that Jesus Christ is 'the Son of God' has centuries of tradition behind it, but may be misleading in a modern context.
- The Fourth Gospel gives us a wider perspective: Jesus is God in action, dying for his people, and offering life beyond death

6

Being Nice to People

The story of how the disciples waited for the coming of the Holy Spirit is described in considerable detail in the Acts of the Apostles, but if Richard Dawkins has read it, it does not appear to have taken root in his mind. A check through the indexes of his books reveals only one reference under 'Holy', and that is to 'Holy War'. In the index to *The God Delusion,* he skips straight from 'Holocaust' to 'Homosexuality'; but what Christians call 'the work of the Holy Spirit' seems to be what he classifies as 'co-operation' or 'altruism' or 'being nice to people'. He thinks that even genes co-operate on occasion, selfish as they are. However, his ideas on the subject and Christian ideas on the subject are so much at variance that they must be treated separately: there is simply no point of contact.

Richard Dawkins on altruism

Richard Dawkins claims that there are sound Darwinian reasons for some degree of co-operation between the genes, as they struggle for survival. They tend to favour their own genetic kin (that is natural selection, protecting the family genes); they do favours for other genes which do favours for them (reciprocal altruism); and sometimes they do favours to other genes to show how superior they are. In *The God*

Delusion, he says that this behaviour is 'not to be thought of as reductive of the noble emotions of compassion and generosity',[1] but the noble emotions are to be found in the animal world. Two chapters in *The Selfish Gene* set out his ideas in some detail. Chapter 10 is called 'You Scratch My Back, I'll Ride On Yours'. In this analysis he starts with bird alarm calls (warning other birds of the approach of danger), and proceeds to ten pages on insects. The passage on the worker bees is not for the squeamish. We are then informed that some birds lick ticks off each other's heads, because they cannot reach the ticks on their own heads, and that mice lick sores on each other's heads for the same reason. This leads to an analysis of three kinds of response. Some mice, birds or other creatures are Cheats: they will accept the service, but not pay it back in kind. The kind bird or mouse is left with his own ticks or sores. Some of them are Suckers: they go on licking other heads although they know they will not get a return for it. Some of them learn to be Grudgers: they help friends and neighbours, but refuse to help Cheats. Richard Dawkins studies the subject of altruism by carrying out computer simulations on populations of insects. He comes to the conclusion that these three responses lead to longer survival. He stops short of extending his observations to human beings. He says:

> There is no end to the fascinating speculation that the idea of reciprocal altruism engenders when we apply it to our own species. Tempting as it is, I am no better at such speculation than the next man, and I leave the reader to entertain himself.

Chapter 12 of *The Selfish Gene* is entitled 'Nice Guys Finish First', but it is not about the noble emotion of compassion. He spends a good 12 pages on games theory, to prove that on the whole, a 'nice' strategy works better than a 'nasty' strategy.

He does mention 'a forgiving strategy', but this is by no means unconditional forgiveness. He equates it with 'Tit for Tat' – a quick retaliation, then forgetting. This sounds very much like 'an eye for an eye and a tooth for a tooth' – the old Mosaic Law, which is still the basis of shariah law. After that, there are two pages of applications to the human situation: one to the painful processes of divorce, and one to football. Then he returns to the vampire bats, whose habits are quite as unpleasant as those of the worker bees. When he is writing about insects, he is reporting actual observations; but when he is writing about human beings, he seems to be writing only from his own personal experience, since he makes no references to sociology or social psychology.

The Christian explanation

Christians think that altruism or 'being nice to people' is very difficult, because we were given free will, and we tend to use it for our own advantage. The Holy Spirit, which came to the disciples at Pentecost or the first Whitsun, is the power which enables us to get beyond selfishness, to work with and care for each other.

The traditional name for the Holy Spirit was 'the Holy Ghost', but it has nothing to do with things that go bump in the night. In the Middle Ages, 'ghost' simply meant a spirit, an invisible presence. Priests gave 'ghostly comfort' to their people, meaning spiritual comfort; but the modern meaning of 'ghost' is a very superstitious one, so 'Holy Spirit' avoids misunderstandings.

Luke the physician tells in the first chapter of the Acts of the Apostles how Jesus' followers gathered together, and the Holy Spirit came upon them.[2] They heard a noise, like that of a hurricane, and they saw something intense and vivid, though they had difficulty in describing what it was. It shook each of them with force. If Luke had known about electricity, he might have said that it was like an electric shock. People said it was as if a fire rushed through the place, setting each of them alight in turn. His account suggests a shattering event – quite unexpected, and causing great excitement.

People who came to see what was happening said that the disciples were telling the news in many different languages, and everybody could understand them. Was this a miracle? Since God invented language, presumably he could make everyone speak Mohican if he wanted to; but if we are looking for a rational explanation, we might speculate that what happened was the sort of crowd emotion people often experience at weddings or funerals or football matches or concerts – beyond words. Or it could have been chiefly a matter of body language. In any case, the people of Jerusalem were polyglot – most of them probably spoke smatterings of half a dozen languages. It would only take a few to say 'Isn't this the group who were followers of the dead carpenter?' for the whole crowd to grasp that something extraordinary was happening.

Peter stood up and explained to the crowd what was happening. He told them that the prophets had forecast the coming of the Spirit, and that Jesus had promised to send it to them.[3] St John's Gospel recounts how Jesus described it to Nicodemus: 'The wind blows where it chooses, and you hear the sound of it, but you do not know where it comes from, or where it goes. So it is with every one who is born of the Spirit.'[4] He promised that the Spirit would guide the disciples into 'all truth'.[5] St Paul says that the Spirit 'searches all things',[6] and urges the Galatians to 'walk in the Spirit'.[7]

To Richard Dawkins, this must sound very vague: just the sort of thing he distrusts; but to the people who experienced it, it was anything but vague. It was shaking and all-encompassing.

Are Christians polytheists?

Christians believe that the Holy Spirit is the spirit of God in the world. It is the Third Person of the Trinity, with God the Creator and Jesus Christ, God in action: it is God working through human beings, and through history.

Richard Dawkins' reaction to this in *The God Delusion* is to accuse Christians of being polytheists.[8] He cannot have been listening to all the sermons he must have heard in the chapel at Oundle. The passage headed 'Polytheism' is very poorly argued. He appears to be saying that Christians are polytheists because they worship three Gods, and that Hindus are monotheists, because all the many Hindu gods are just different manifestations or incarnations of the one God, Brahma. He is not much of a guide on comparative religion. Has he ever talked seriously to Hindus or visited a Hindu temple? There is an absolute pantheon of Hindu gods. In a Hindu temple in Madras, there is a statue of St Thomas, who is said to have made a missionary journey across the Indian ocean. He appears in company with several hundred Hindu deities,[9] because the hospitable Hindus adopted him. Christianity, like Judaism and Islam, has always preached that there is one God; but Christians recognize that God has three different kinds of activity. We are used to thinking of 'persons' as distinct individuals, separate from one another; but God is suprapersonal. The nearest we can get to that idea is in love for another person, that takes us beyond self-centredness into a relationship. Two people become a couple, or in popular terms 'an item'. God is Three in One and One in Three.

The Trinity is not a committee. God the Creator, Jesus Christ who came to earth and God the Holy Spirit are different aspects of our one God, not different people sitting round a table.

In the early centuries of the Christian era, trying to work this out caused agonized and heated debate. The relationship between the Creator and Jesus Christ was understood as that of the Father and the Son, one 'begetting' and the other 'begotten'. That was framed in the terms of the patriarchal society the Fathers of the Church understood; but when it came to the Holy Spirit, this simple analogy broke down. The Creator-Father did not have two sons. Over the centuries, there have been protracted theological debates about how to describe the relationship of the Holy Spirit with the other two.

Artists have had great problems in painting the Holy Trinity. Medieval paintings usually portray God the Creator as a bearded figure on his throne, Christ on the cross, and the Spirit as a dove, hovering above the other two. The dove was a reminder of the early story in Genesis of Noah and the Flood. When the waters subsided, a dove is traditionally said to have come to Noah, symbolizing peace and hope.[10]

Spreading the Gospel

We can only judge the truth of Luke's account by looking at the results. The original band of rather disheartened disciples dramatically gained a new strength, and began the spread of Christ's message. At first they thought it was only for Jews. The Jews always had a very sharp sense of being different from the people round them. Jesus Christ himself thought that he had come to minister only to the Jews, until that Canaanite woman said that even the dogs could lick up the crumbs from under the table. Then he realized that his mission was much wider than that. Later, he charged his disciples, 'Go therefore and make disciples of all nations',[11] and said, 'I have other sheep, which do not belong to this fold';[12] but the disciples still thought of themselves as a distinctively Jewish group. Then they began to realize that the Holy Spirit could be passed on to Gentiles as well. The disciple Philip baptized an Ethiopian he met on the road through the wilderness between Jerusalem and Gaza.[13] Peter had a dream or a vision, and came to realize that the complicated rules about diet that all Jews followed did not have to apply to people of other cultural backgrounds.[14] He and Paul had a long argument about whether male converts ought to be circumcised, as all Jewish males were, and came to the conclusion that circumcision was not necessary.[15] So they set out to tell the rest of the known world about the Holy Spirit.

They put their lives on the line. Most of them were eventually killed for trying to preach their message. The Holy Spirit made such a marked difference to their behaviour, endowed them with such courage and conviction, that someone tried to buy it, like vitamin pills. A sorcerer called Simon Magus offered Peter money for the 'secret' of power; but there was no secret. Peter told him that his heart was not right before God; and Simon Magus became a Christian.[16] If this story was fiction, he would probably have been struck by a thunderbolt.

Richard Dawkins says 'Christianity was founded by Paul of Tarsus',[17] and 'It was Paul who invented the idea of taking the Jewish God to the Gentiles.'[18] He adduces no evidence for these statements. Paul is not mentioned in the Four Gospels. He did not even meet Jesus Christ during his earthly life. In the early days of the Church, he was working for the Temple authorities against the Christians. He was present at the stoning of Stephen, the first martyr, and was on his way to Damascus to root out the Christians there when he had a vision – or an attack of conscience, or some say an epileptic fit, which can produce a period of unusual mental clarity afterwards. After that, he joined the Church, but some of the Jerusalem Christians were very suspicious and thought he was a spy.[19]

The Acts of the Apostles tell in detail how Paul travelled

round the Mediterranean. Luke was with him for much of the time. John Mark and Bartholomew accompanied him to Cyprus and other eastern Mediterranean cities. Nearly all the apostles were eventually martyred. James the Great was killed in Jerusalem on the orders of Herod, but most of the others died in foreign places: Matthew in Ethiopia, Mark in Alexandria, Andrew in Greece, Thomas possibly in India, Bartholomew in Cyprus, Peter and Paul in Rome in the persecutions of Nero.

What the Holy Spirit did for them was to give them the insight and the strength to preach a radically new message to a brutal and violent world: a message of peace and fellowship and mercy; and the courage to die for it.

The Holy Spirit in the early Church

What is the Holy Spirit like, and what does it do? We live in a visual age, with television, digital cameras, mobile tele-cameras and CCTV, so we tend to want visual proof of everything, preferably in 30 seconds; but we do have a description of what the Holy Spirit is like in an Old Testament prophecy. In the book of Isaiah, it is forecast that the spirit of the Lord which would come through the Messiah would be 'the spirit of wisdom and understanding, the spirit of counsel and might, the spirit of knowledge and the fear of the Lord'.[20] 'Counsel' appears to mean something like 'good judgement', and 'might' is the power to act. 'The fear of the Lord' is not fear in the ordinary sense of the term, but something closer to reverence for God. These are the six gifts of the Holy Spirit. The 'fruits' or results of the Holy Spirit are described by St Paul. He tells the Galatians 'the fruit of the Spirit is love, joy, peace, patience, kindness, generosity, faithfulness, gentleness and self-control'.[21] As the story of Simon Magus tells us, it was not magic. Christians were always clear that the Holy Spirit had to be received with an open heart and mind, and that it was very wrong to try to manipulate it, or to seek it for the wrong purposes; but the Holy Spirit was the power that kept Christians witnessing and prepared to die for their faith through more than 250 years of persecution by the Roman authorities.

Many historical sources, ancient and modern, testify to their bravery in great detail. Christianity came from the remote Eastern provinces, and Christians were opposed to the brutalities and inanities of Roman culture; but there were some very dark cults and curious beliefs washing around the Mediterranean basin, and it was easy to represent Christianity as one of the undesirable ones. Some Roman emperors (Nero, Hadrian, Severus, Diocletian in particular) regarded Christianity as un-Roman, anti-social and probably subversive. It was a religion brought by despised people from conquered lands – Jews and Greeks. The Jews were thought of as awkward people with their own curious customs, and the Greeks in Italy, though often more literate than their Roman masters, were mostly slaves. Christians were rumoured to practise a secret rite, involving the body and blood of a dead carpenter. Rumours flourished: they were said to practise black magic, to eat babies, to raise corpses from the dead.

Most Roman citizens probably had little faith in the Roman gods, and were privately cynical; but the worship of the gods was the device that held Roman society together in public ceremonial: a kind of social cement. Several of the emperors seem to have become convinced that they were gods themselves, so they were prepared to use total brutality to wipe out this alien cult. It was not until the time of the Emperor Constantine, in the early fourth century, that the persecutions were stopped.

Then the Church became respectable. Constantine was a

soldier and the ruler of an enormous empire. He probably had little time for theological speculation; but he allowed freedom of worship throughout the Empire, and he was very generous to the Church. He built the first St Peter's in Rome, carrying 12 baskets of rubbish down the hill with his own hands in memory of the 12 apostles. He endowed the papacy; and he rebuilt the churches founded on the site of the Nativity and the Holy Sepulchre in the Holy Land, in magnificent fashion.[22] The mosaic floor which he commissioned for the Church of the Holy Nativity is still there today.

After Constantine, the Christian Church became a major social institution. It had been tested by persecution, dispersal and martyrdom. Now it was to be tested by power, privilege and magnificence; but the first step was to put its house in order. Pope Damasus I, who held the pontificate from 366 to 384, is credited with the main work of organizing the commemoration of the Christians of the earlier period. He commissioned excavations to find and honour the bones of the martyrs. The bishops of the Church were summoned, and set to work on defining what Christians believed[23] and which of the accounts of the life of Christ and the missions of his disciples should be authorized and translated from Greek into Latin. Much of this work was carried out by his secretary, Jerome or Hieronymus. The first list of the saints of the Church is known as the *Hieronymianum*. After the death of Pope Damasus, Jerome continued to work on translations of both the Old and the New Testament. His immense labours produced most of what became recognized as the Vulgate, the official version of the Bible which went unchallenged until the Reformation of the sixteenth century.

Lost gospels?

In recent years, a number of writers have taken up the sugges-
tion made by Dan Brown in *The Da Vinci Code* that the
Church deliberately suppressed the truth of the life of Jesus
for nearly 2,000 years, substituting a false official version.
This is simply untrue. It is true that there were many documents claiming to tell all or part of the story of the life of
Jesus, and not all were officially approved by the early Church.
It is also true that further documents of this kind were
unearthed during archaeological excavations in the late nineteenth and early twentieth centuries, and remained similarly
unapproved. From the time of the resurrection, many people
had been trying to write accounts of the extraordinary things
that had happened, and some of these were of better quality
than others. From the earliest days, the Church was concerned
to preserve the real gospel stories, and to stop people from
embroidering and inventing new marvels. In particular, they
had trouble with the Gnostics, a mystical sect with Zoroastrian
(Persian) roots, who were producing stories about the life of
Christ as early as the second century. In the second century –
long before Constantine – the Gnostics thought that Christians
had a secret wisdom that was only for the elect, and embel-
lished the plain facts with visions and esoteric marvels. Bishop
Irenaus of Lyons[24] wrote a remarkable work, *Adversus
Haereses*, 'Against the Heretics', to expose the distortions in
their thinking. Irenaeus called it 'stripping the fox', and he
was one of the earliest scholars to try to safeguard the true
story of Jesus Christ's life from the many fanciful accounts
being written and circulated round the Middle East at that
time. Irenaeus was a passionate believer in truth, and a really
astringent thinker. If Richard Dawkins had read *Adversus
Haereses*, it might have changed his opinion that all Christians
are 'dyed in the wool faith-heads'.

Richard Dawkins says that the Gospels are ancient fiction, and *The Da Vinci Code* is modern fiction;[25] but the Gospels are not fiction. An Oxford don married to a scriptwriter ought to be able to tell the difference between fact and fiction by the method he himself recommends: studying the evidence. He is quite right in saying that repeating a story over and over again for centuries does not make it true. On the other hand, if he had looked seriously at the Acts of the Apostles – Peter's speech to the crowds at Pentecost[26] or Stephen's very learned and scholarly defence when he was arraigned before the Sanhedrin[27] – he would surely have recognized the bite of truth. Those are reports of inspired speeches by eye-witnesses of the events they describe. Similarly, Luke's long accounts of Paul's journeys round the Mediterranean inspire confidence: they are travel diaries. The routes can be checked, and the traditions are still alive in the places they visited. The New Testament Epistles or Letters are genuine letters to real people; and all written in the first century, most before Peter and Paul died in Nero's persecutions in AD 64/65.

The story of the 'lost gospels' seems to have been given publicity by *The Da Vinci Code*, in which it is alleged that Jesus Christ married Mary Magdalene. This is pure fiction, and even Richard Dawkins does not waste time on it; but it was the beginning of a remarkable exercise in theological spin. It is based on some medieval romances culled from an earlier book entitled *Holy Blood, Holy Grail*.[28] The allegation is said to be contained in an ancient document called *The Gospel of Mary* which was suppressed, and only came to light recently. In fact, *The Gospel of Mary* was discovered in 1898. Scholars have known about it for over a century, and it says absolutely nothing about Jesus marrying Mary Magdalene or anyone else. It is written on papyrus. The manuscript is written in an ancient Coptic dialect, and it is not complete. It consists of nine pages out of an original nineteen.

The manuscript comes from an area of Upper Egypt where many Christians went for safety during the persecutions – a long way from Jerusalem. Carbon dating and other techniques date it to the third century, but it may be based on older material. It was deposed in the Egyptian Department of the National Museum in Berlin, where it is known as Papyrus Berolinensis 8502, or the Berlin Codex. It has long been available for scholars, but it was not published in English until 1977.[29]

In this document, Mary is said to have told the apostles of a dream in which the risen Christ communicated secret wisdom to her – on such matters as the seven powers of Wrath, including Darkness, Desire, Ignorance and the Foolish Learning of Flesh. This is typical Gnostic writing – familiar enough to anyone who has read other Gnostic accounts. It lacks the immediacy and veracity of the eye-witness accounts from Jerusalem. Biblical scholars do not consider it a serious work.

The garbled accounts in *Holy Blood, Holy Grail* and *The Da Vinci Code* have led to a wider interest in 'lost gospels', which encourages Richard Dawkins to dismiss all the Gospels, including those in the New Testament, as fiction. There are other works of this kind: *The Gospel of Thomas*,[30] *The Apocalypse of Peter*, *The Secret Gospel of Mark*, *The Gospel of Philip*, *The Acts of Paul and Thecla*, *The First Gospel of the Infancy of Jesus*, *The Protogospel of James* and a number of others.[31] They are all available in good theological libraries. These are what are called 'apocryphal gospels'. Some tell unlikely and pointless miracles, some include myths and legends, most attract comments from biblical scholars like 'clumsy', 'tasteless' and 'dubious'.

It is only recently that the general public has become interested in these texts. In a television programme just before Christmas 2006,[32] an Anglican priest with long hair, wearing jeans and a slouch hat and a neckerchief – looking, as one TV critic said at the time, like Indiana Jones – was photographed walking about the Bible lands and telling viewers that the failure of the Church to approve these accounts was 'shocking'. He alleged that 'the Church authorities condemned a wealth of literature'; but these works were never 'condemned'. They were not approved because they were thought to be of poor quality – written long after the events by people who had no knowledge of what actually occurred. Many of them, like *The Gospel of Mary*, are of Gnostic origin.

The Da Vinci Code was a runaway bestseller, largely because of all the codes and puzzles. Dan Brown said that his motto was 'Location, location, location', and travel agents have started tours to the Louvre, the Temple church and other sites mentioned in the book, in the hope of finding non-existent clues. The whole business of the 'lost gospels' has been a money-spinner, not a contribution to biblical scholarship.

The authorized New Testament

Richard Dawkins says that people are not used to answering questions like who wrote the New Testament and when.[33] That may be true in departments of zoology, but it is certainly not true of New Testament scholars. He also says that the Gospels were 'chosen more or less arbitrarily'. They were not. The final selection was made in the terms in which the authenticity of documents is always considered – the work of Shakespeare, Mao Tse Tung or any author you care to name. Who wrote it? How do we know? Where was it written? Why was it written? Does the writer have an axe to grind? Does it tell us anything new or valuable? Can we check the facts in other writings of the same period? Above all, is this a truthful witness? No documents can have been subjected to longer and more sustained critical scrutiny.

Richard Dawkins cannot have looked at the facts of how the original versions of the New Testament were carefully preserved as precious documents, and then translated and copied. In the late third century, Jerome, the Pope's own secretary, with all the resources of the Church to draw on, went back to the earliest texts that could then be located and translated them afresh from Greek and Hebrew with the aid of translators, transcribers and other assistants. After the death of Pope Damasus (Jerome narrowly missed being elected Pope himself), he moved to Bethlehem, the place where it all began, and worked there in a cave next to the cave of the nativity. Visitors can still go to his cave.[34] He worked steadily there for some 30 years, and produced the text of the Vulgate, which was accepted throughout Christendom until the Reformation, and is still the basis of Roman Catholic versions of the Bible. Then Protestant writers went back to the early Greek and Hebrew texts again to check Jerome's version. Like Irenaeus, Jerome was not concerned to distort the story of Jesus' life, only to clear it of errors and to tell it truthfully.

The manuscripts are not 'cobbled together', but carefully selected as the truest account of the events they describe. They were very carefully copied without editing or distortion. Exact copying was certainly more difficult in the days before the photocopier; but in the monastery libraries and scriptoria where the work was carried out, tremendous efforts were taken to get the copies accurate and exact. People knew the difference between a good copy and a flawed one. Faithful copies were highly prized, and good copyists regarded as possessing a vital skill. The Bible texts have been protected ever since, and endlessly analysed and tested, particularly since the development of spectal imaging and other modern techniques.

The Holy Spirit in history

Christianity, like Islam, is an historically based religion, so Christians keep contact with their historical roots. History is not a moving spotlight to us, but a searchlight – the source of a continuous stream of information and understanding.

The difficulty was that, as the Church became wealthy and protected by emperors and princes, it also became authoritarian and much too sure of itself. Max Weber's monumental work *On Charisma and Institution Building* analyses what happens to social institutions when they grow in size and power. Whether they are nation-states or religious groups or local clubs, they have to grow or die. If they grow, they tend to move from a first stage where they are inspired by a charismatic individual to a bureaucratic stage where they become unwieldy and self-serving, and eventually dictatorial.

Though the Church is a very unusual institution, it is not exempt from the laws of social dynamics. Though most Church leaders conscientiously try to seek the guidance of the Holy Spirit, it *is* an institution, and they are only fallible humans, so sometimes in their anxiety to get things right, they get them very wrong. After Constantine, the Church acquired an unprecedented hold over nearly all Europe. It framed rules, and the rules became increasingly complex: who was a member and who was not, what people were allowed to pray for and in what words, who could become a priest, which priests were senior to other priests. It became centralized and authoritarian. The popes – bishops of the Church of Rome – claimed to be the successors of St Peter, and to exact conformity from all the churches based in Alexandria, Athens, Ephesus, Antioch, Constantinople and other mission centres.

The basis of this claim has been much debated. In Matthew's Gospel – but not the other three Gospels – Jesus Christ is reported as saying, 'You are Peter, and on this rock I will build my church.'[35] In Greek, 'Peter' is *Cephas*, which means a rock, so that was originally a pun. There are different interpretations of this text. Roman Catholics believe that St Peter was commissioned to found the whole Christian Church, and became the first pope. The present pope is thus his successor, the spiritual head of the whole Christian Church. Christ's statement 'Thou art Peter . . .' is inscribed in Latin round the inner circle of the dome of St Peter's Church in Rome, in a claim to unbroken succession for 2,000 years; but in the enormous literature on the papacy, scholars can identify all sorts of hiccups in the process: disputed elections, scandal-mongering campaigns, power brokering, rival candidates both claiming the papacy at once. The basic difference between Roman Catholics and other Christians is that Roman Catholics, having in some sense inherited the centralizing ethos of the Roman Empire, think that unity in the name of the Holy Spirit is more important than differences of attitude and interpretation, while other Christians maintain that the Holy Spirit can work through such differences.

An organization – any organisation – grows at the periphery, where it comes into contact with outside influences, not at the centre.

Anglicans and members of the Free Churches (apart from those who do not believe in bishops) respect the pope as a bishop, but not as the supreme authority. The Eastern Orthodox Church similarly maintains its own traditions from the area where Christianity began. Was 'Thou art Peter' and the pun about the rock a clear directive that the Holy Spirit would operate through a single channel? Or was it more personal, an affectionate recognition that Christ's sturdy friend and ally would play a leading part in the development of his mission?

Successive popes have seen their main task as preserving 'the Faith' intact in a single organizational structure; but the Vatican does increasingly have relations with other faith communities – Jews, Anglicans, Eastern Orthodox and so on. There are now many avenues for inter-faith discussion, and a new spirit of tolerance The real arguments between faith groups are often about authority and management style, rather than about the nature of faith itself.

So in all the divisions, where is the Holy Spirit? Christian life would be a great deal simpler if the churches infallibly produced the Fruits of the Spirit – love, joy, peace, patience, kindness, generosity, faithfulness, gentleness and self-control; but of course there is a catch: the Holy Spirit does not act like some sort of spiritual Persil or Daz; and the operation of the Spirit of Truth is often painful. It involves co-operation and tolerance and much more than 'being nice to people'.

Do we need the Church?

Richard Dawkins focuses his attack in *The God Delusion* on the Roman Catholic Church, and has little or nothing to say about other churches.[36] He thinks that the Church is unnecessary: human beings are well able to practise 'altruism' without it. He notes how, among 'the large number of letters from readers of my books', some are 'enthusiastically friendly', some are 'helpfully critical', but those which are 'nasty or even vicious', subjecting him to attacks of 'unchristian abuse' are from Christians. From the tone of the letters which he reproduces, they come from a few very unbalanced and possibly dangerous individuals, and are scarcely evidence of the general attitude of Christians to his own attacks on their faith. As he admits in several places, bishops and theologians seem to have been courteous and co-operative in their discussions with him; but he uses these extracts from his fan mail only as preliminaries to the general question: 'Why, I can't help wondering, is God thought to need such ferocious defence?'

Goodness, he argues, is not dependent on belief in God:

Do you really mean to tell me that the only reason you try to be good is to gain God's approval and rewards? Or to avoid his disapproval and punishment? That's just sucking up, apple-polishing, looking over your shoulder at the great surveillance camera in the sky, or the still small wiretap in your head, monitoring your every move, even your every base thought.

He thinks our moral sense has a Darwinian origin: the Good Samaritan in us is not incompatible with the 'selfish gene'. He displays a sunny trust in human nature, asking 'Do we really need policing?' Half an hour with an Oxford criminologist or the nearest police constable might answer that question for him. Does he know nothing of organized crime, of the drug culture and the prevalence of knives and guns? Or of the urban ghettos where ASBOs are handed out as frequently as parking tickets?

Richard Dawkins argues that people can be 'moral' without any help from the Church or other religious organizations; but many millions of people do not agree with him. They think that being good is a life against nature, not a development from the animal world, and that it is very difficult for human beings, just because we are born selfish. In spite of all we have seen through the centuries of its divisions, its inadequacy, its bigotry and its pretensions, the Christian Church in its different forms is still the central means of spreading Christ's gospel – a rope for Christians to grasp as they stumble through life: sometimes stained, sometimes dismayingly frayed, but a channel for the operation of the Holy Spirit.

Is it necessary to be a member of the Church to call on the help of the Holy Spirit? Jesus Christ told the disciples that the Spirit blows where it chooses. They had to learn that it was not limited by distinctive Jewish customs like diet and circumcision. In the present generation, living more closely with people of other faiths, other cultures and other values, we have come increasingly to realize that the Holy Spirit is not confined to recognized channels. We cannot hold it captive in our human-made structures. God created and cares for the whole world.

What Christians believe is complicated: a single God known to us through three 'Persons' or aspects, a God who does not just sit and wait for people to do as he says, but who came down to show us how to do it; a Spirit we cannot see and cannot analyse, which blows where it likes. It takes some working out. And the Church has so often got it wrong – developing fixed formularies for belief, and then threatening unbelievers with hellfire and damnation; suppressing free enquiry and free speech; claiming to save people's souls with the rack and the thumbscrew; burning them alive for the good of their souls.

No wonder that Richard Dawkins asks how Christians can possibly defend these practices. Of course, we cannot defend the terrible cruelties practised in the name of religion in the past. These are totally indefensible. There are terrible stains on the history of the Church. Did the Church authorities really believe that they were keeping the faith pure by assaulting bodies to bend minds? Did they really believe that torture and the threat of execution would save the heretic's soul by leading him or her to recant? All that panoply of power and hatred is nothing short of grotesque – and it was carried out in the name of Jesus Christ, who never hurt anyone; but if we are looking for explanations of the evils of the Crusades and the wars of religion, we must go beyond the issue of whether this kind of mass psychosis is labelled religious or not, and look for answers at a deeper level. The causes of human conflict are much more complex than Richard Dawkins suggests.

Key points

- Richard Dawkins' views on altruism appear to be largely drawn from computer simulations of the behaviour of insects, and he is reluctant to apply them to human behaviour.
- Christians draw their views on the subject from the Acts of the Apostles, which describe the coming and the operation of the Holy Spirit.
- The Holy Spirit is the Spirit of Truth, the Third Person of the Holy Trinity, working through history.
- The New Testament accounts of the work of the early Christians are fact, not fiction. They have been carefully preserved, analysed and subjected to repeated scrutiny for nearly 2,000 years. The so-called 'lost gospels' are later works which do not carry the same authority.
- Though the Church has often been led into intolerance and cruelty in the past in its attempt to preserve and promote its message, it is not responsible for all the evils with which Richard Dawkins charges it. These require a more sophisticated analysis.

7

Imagine . . .

Morality has existed 'ever since *Homo erectus* stood up and looked at the sun', according to Richard Dawkins, but this claim cannot be put to the test. If the 'African Eve' existed, we have very little idea what she looked like 45,000 years ago, and how far she resembled a modern human or a modern chimpanzee. He goes on to argue, '*if* our moral sense, like our sexual desire, is indeed rooted deep in our Darwinian past, pre-dating religion . . .',[1] but 'if' is the operative word. What evidence can he produce that morality is rooted deep in our Darwinian past? Only computer simulations of the behaviour of those birds and mice that lick each other's heads.

If he thinks that this limited kind of morality is innate, he also knows that the religious instinct is innate. All human societies have some sort of religion, based on that sense of 'wonder' that he himself experiences; but he does not see any connection between innate morality and innate religious instinct. The recognition of religious instinct merely provokes him to another of his strings of adjectives: 'No known culture lacks some version of the time-consuming, wealth-consuming, hostility-provoking rituals, the anti-factual, counter-productive fantasies of religion.'[2] By 'counter-productive' he apparently means that religion does not contribute to the survival of genes – the only form of evolution he is prepared to recognize.

Is religion the primary cause of conflict?

As he makes clear in *The God Delusion*, Richard Dawkins regards religion as a highly dangerous and anti-social force. Here is his full list of indictments,[3] numbered for ease of reference. Without religion, he says, there would be:

1 No suicide bombers
2 No 9/11
3 No 7/7
4 No Crusades
5 No witch-hunts
6 No Gunpowder Plot
7 No Indian partition
8 No Israeli–Palestinian war.
9 No Serb/Croat/Muslim massacres
10 No persecution of Jews as 'Christ-killers'
11 No Northern Ireland 'troubles'
12 No 'honour killings'
13 No shiny-suited bouffant-haired televangelists
14 No Taliban to blow up ancient statues
15 No public beheadings of blasphemers
16 No 'flogging of female skin for the crime of showing an inch of it'.

There are some notable omissions from this list, including all the major conflicts of the twentieth century: Nazi concentration camps, Stalinist pogroms, Pol Pot, the Mau Mau, and many other cruel and oppressive regimes had nothing whatever to do with religion. We might conclude that societies that reject religion are no closer to peace and harmony than those that accept it.

The list consists of 16 separate indictments. They are not presented either chronologically or thematically. They span over nearly a thousand years – from the first Crusade to the London Underground bombings of 2005 and more recent suicide bombers. Eleven items – numbers 1, 2, 3, 4, 7, 8, 9, 13, 14, 15 and 16 – relate to conflicts between Islamic societies (or individuals) and the West. These are deep-seated, and have more than a thousand years of history behind them. They involve many different issues – cultural, political, economic. Only five items on his list refer to aggression in Western societies. Of these, the witch-hunts are long since over. It is more than 400 years since the Gunpowder Plot – and surely planning to blow up the House of Commons was a political act? Most people know that the persecution of the Jews in the Middle Ages was not because they were 'Christ-killers'. It was because the medieval Church forbade usury – the lending of money for interest – and so the Jews became the bankers of Europe. From time to time, the Jews got too rich, the kings and princes and bishops got too poor, and the Jews were persecuted or driven out to square the books.[4] The accusation that the Jews were 'Christ-killers' may have been bandied about as a justification, but it never made any sort of sense. Jesus Christ and his disciples were Jews, too.

The only remaining items on his list are Northern Ireland and the televangelists, items 11 and 13. Televangelists are a matter of viewing taste, whether their suits are shiny or not. The 'Troubles' in Northern Ireland – the Irish always give them a capital T – are a much more serious matter; but the subsequent discussion in *The God Delusion* suggests a number of causes of conflict other than religious causes. It is only in the headline-grabbing early pages that Richard Dawkins puts all the blame on religion. After this early exercise in dogmatism, he retreats to a much less extreme position.

Political and economic causes of conflict

He does not appear to have any personal experience of terrorism in Northern Ireland,[5] but when he comes to consider the
issues in depth, he concedes that Irish terrorists did not have
theological disagreements with their victims. In *A Devil's
Chaplain*, he says: 'They are killing because the other lot
killed their father, or because the other lot drove their great-
grandfathers off their land, or because the other lot oppressed
our lot economically for centuries.'[6] The main motives for
conflict are revenge, territorialism and poverty.

The basic problems in Northern Ireland have long been
ethnic and economic. The Republicans ('Catholics') are
Celtic stock. The Unionists ('Protestants') were immigrants
from Scotland in the centuries of domination from mainland
Britain. Republicans have long memories – they will recount
how successive English kings and their armies, from Edward
I on, invaded their territory, burned their homes and their
crops, stole their land and left their children to starve. They
will recall how Cromwell stabbed them in the back. They
will describe the Great Famine of the 1840s, when the potato
harvest failed and thousands died of hunger; and what it
was like, right up to the 1970s, to live in a country where
the soldiers, the policemen, the prison officers, the clerks in
the benefit office and the housing officers were all Unionists,
and the people in need were nearly all Republicans. Richard
Dawkins notes that the divisions still come out in football
– Celtic v. Rangers is always a gladiatorial contest. He says
'They might belong to different species.' They do.

Labelling

Richard Dawkins notes that in Northern Ireland, 'Catholic' and 'Protestant' are labels, easily attached, difficult to change. He comments that to see the dispute in terms of religious labels is 'not necessarily worse than (using) other labels, such as skin colour, language or preferred football teams', and religious labels are 'often available when other labels are not'. Labels are useful to the media, which often speak in headlines, useful in popular speech, but frequently misleading. He asks for plain and direct speech, saying, 'If it's a spade we have here, let's call it a spade.'[7]

In spite of this excellent intention, he goes on to blame 'religion' alone for the carnage of 9/11. He says in *A Devil's Chaplain* that his 'last respect for religion' vanished in the smoke and choking dust of the Twin Towers. As with the 'Troubles' in Northern Ireland, he is not speaking from personal experience, because he was not there at the time. Dr Rowan Williams, Archbishop of Canterbury, was in New York on that day, close enough to inhale the smoke and the dust. He wrote an honest and painful book on the experience,[8] and came to very different conclusions, which offer hope for the human capacity to heal. Richard Dawkins can only speak of 'bitter sectarian hatred' – 'Is there no catastrophe terrible enough to shake the faith of people, on both sides, in God's goodness and power?'[9] Despite all his protestations, he is still not looking beyond the label to the complex causes of human aggression.

Group loyalties and group hostilities

Yet in *The God Delusion*, he writes: 'I do not deny that humanity's powerful tendencies towards group loyalties and out-group hostilities would exist even in the absence of religion.'[10] He does not develop this theme; but it is one worth developing if we are to understand the processes to which he is referring.

In many bitter conflicts that have traditionally been classified under a religious label, whole groups of people – whole villages, whole towns, whole countries – have been seized by fear of people they did not understand, and have reacted with irrational aggression. At any time from the Crusades through to the Witches of Salem in the seventeenth century, people in Western Europe believed that they were fighting the powers of darkness, the devil himself. In the growing rationalism of the eighteenth century, they came to realize that many of the so-called witches were harmless – wandering vagabonds, social misfits, demented old women, hysterical girls: anybody who seemed odd and failed to keep to the conventions of the time.

In the terms of social psychology, the Other can equally be a traitor, a criminal, a foreigner: somebody who is not part of one's own social group, someone whose motivation is thought to be hostile.[11] Sigmund Freud taught us in *Group Psychology and the Analysis of the Ego* how the in-group defends itself against the out-group. The group mobilizes all the positive emotions – love, loyalty, friendship, trust – for its own support, and projects all the negative emotions – suspicion, hatred, violence – on to any group that seems to threaten its identity.

Does this still happen today? We might note that sections of the British press have not been exactly positive about Roumanians and Bulgarians recently. They are represented as coming into 'our' country, destroying 'our' way of life. Though key concepts in Freudian analysis, such as 'primal horde' theory and Oedipal theory, have come to be regarded as highly debatable by many practitioners in recent years, Freud's understanding of the basic principles of group dynamics has been widely recognized in the social sciences, and forms the basis of much current work in conflict resolution.

The instinct to protect the group seems to be the result of very powerful basic drives. Scratch the surface, and you will find the same sort of mixed motivation in conflicts labelled 'religious' as in outbreaks of murderous violence that are attributed to secular causes: the desire to control territory, secure borders, manage scarce resources; individual ambition – the desire to be powerful, dominate others, make money. Religious terminology has often been invoked to legitimize violence and inhumanity in situations where the real motive is simple human aggression: so much more dangerous in the modern world than animal aggression.

A world without religion?

Richard Dawkins does not think that religion is entirely an evil influence. He even admits that it has been of benefit to human society in some ways. He would like to keep sacred books on the school syllabus, conceding that they may have some literary value. He also thinks that we 'can retain a sentimental loyalty to the cultural and literary traditions of, say, Judaism, Anglicanism or Islam without buying in to the supernatural beliefs that historically went along with those traditions'; and he would be sorry if we lost Mecca, York Minster, Chartres, Notre Dame, the temples of Kyoto, and the Grand Mosque at Cordoba. He is appalled at the 'unspeakable vandalism' of the Taliban in dynamiting the 150ft high Bamiyan Buddhas.[12] In a word, he wants the artistic results of religious belief without the belief – even though he thinks that the belief is meaningless, and the work a by-product of the evolutionary instinct. He thinks that natural selection explains other human instincts, but not the instinct that led to the building of great places of worship, or the writing of sacred texts.

Nor (and this worries him) does natural selection provide an explanation of compassion to strangers: 'Natural selection has nothing to offer an orphaned child weeping, an old widow in despair from loneliness, an animal whimpering in pain.'[13] Yet we do respond. There is a bit of the Good Samaritan in all of us, and evidently in Richard Dawkins too. How does he explain these unproductive activities? He thinks that the Darwinian imperative has 'misfired', made mistakes: 'Blessed, precious mistakes', he calls them.[14]

This really is a tortuous argument. First, he insists on the existence of a ruthless and over-riding life principle; then he asserts that it includes some form of 'Darwinian' morality; then he recognizes that this is not a sufficient explanation for altruism, and says that altruism is the result of 'mistakes' in which the selfish gene is really acting against its own interests. Finally he says that he is thankful for the mistakes!

Has he really imagined what a twenty-first-century world with 'no religion' would be like? There would be no hospitals, no hospices. There would be no literacy, no universities, no libraries. All these features of society started from Christian origins. There would be no charity. He wants to found his own atheists' charity, but when it comes to wrenching compassion, charitable organizations with religious titles have a long head start.

What would we retain in the artistic world without the religious impulse? Jackson Pollock, Tracey Emin and Damien Hirst would still grace our galleries, but we would have lost Duccio, Michaelangelo, Raphael, Giotto, El Greco, Bellini, Zurburàn . . . most of the great painters and sculptors of the past. It is frequently argued that they chose religious subjects because they were not allowed to paint anything else, but the subjects clearly inspired them. What would they have painted without the great Christian themes? What has secular architecture produced by the early years of the twenty-first century?

The Gherkin? The Millennium Dome? The Pompidou Centre in Paris?

Validating human rights

Richard Dawkins admits that there has been an enormous advance in moral and ethical standards through the centuries. He thinks that this has taken place in spite of religious influences, and his explanation for this change is merely that 'the *Zeitgeist* has moved on'.[15] This is really no explanation at all. Invoking the Spirit of the Age does not tell us why it moves on, or in what direction; but he does note the effects of change. In the Western world at least, we have accepted ideas of gender equality and racial equality that would have been unthinkable even 50 years ago. We no longer call foreigners names like Frog, Wop, Dago, Hun, Yid, Coon, Nip or Wog.[16]

The existence of this change is easy enough to see. Many organizations, religious and secular, are now engaged in working for peace and justice all over the world, at every level from the local to the national and international. Human rights are the subject of international charters and national legislation. In the West, a network of health and social services has developed in country after country to meet the needs of citizens. The United Nations is attempting to establish these rights all round the world. Its efforts are often inadequate, but even the existence of the United Nations would have been unthinkable 150 years ago – that would take us back to the days of Palmerston, and gun-boats up the Yangtse. The armed forces spend much of their time these days acting in co-operation with units from other countries – policing, establishing water supplies and power lines and mending oil pipes, securing supplies – often as part of a combined United Nations or NATO force. There *is* a change of heart. Not universal, not always successful, but light years away from traditional attitudes

Richard Dawkins asks, 'Where have these concerted and steady changes in social consciousness come from?' and comments, 'The onus is not on me to answer. For my purposes, it is sufficient to say that they have certainly not come from religion.' In fact, that is precisely where they have come from. Some writers on human rights argue that the principles can be traced back to classical Greek society, the cradle of democracy; but in the world of Plato and Aristotle, slavery was taken for granted, unfit babies were left to die on the nearest mountain top, and handicapped people were publicly ridiculed. Democratic participation in public affairs was limited to arms-bearing male Athenians. There was not much wrenching compassion in Athens.

Some people trace human rights back to the American Declaration of Independence in 1776. In the Capitol in Washington DC, Thomas Jefferson's draft of the Declaration is displayed in a glass case. 'We hold these truths to be self-evident', and they were defined as the rights to life, liberty and the pursuit of happiness; but Jefferson had black slaves on his estate, and one of them was his long-term mistress. His belief in the Rights of Man did not include blacks, and it did not include women. Jefferson was an agnostic. Richard Dawkins quotes him repeatedly – his dislike of the God of the Old Testament, his disbelief in the Virgin Birth, his ridicule of the concept of the Trinity.[17] Perhaps he is not aware of his hero's blind spots.

The real origin to the human rights movement is to be found not on a hill in Athens or a hill in Washington DC, but in the Gospels. Only Christianity tells us what finger-printing suggested and DNA confirms: that each of us – all the untold millions of human beings right through the ages – is unique and valuable. There is only one Richard Dawkins. Without religion, the life of man (and woman) would have been nasty, solitary, brutish and short – as it was when the ape descendants originally came down from the trees.

The new toleration of the Other is not some unexplained *Zeitgeist*. The 'truths' of human rights are not true at all unless we base them on something more than mere assertion. Book after book has been written on the contention that human rights are 'inalienable',[18] but that is meaningless unless the statement is justified. Cruelty is wrong. Violence is wrong. Treating people – any people, male or female, black or white, rich or poor, old or young, fit or disabled, foreign or native born – as less than human is deeply wrong. That message comes from the Gospels, and there is no other philosophical justification for the growing opposition to racism, sexism, ageism, disablism and all the other isms.

Human rights involve toleration of the Other, and we are having to use a new vocabulary to avoid the stigmatizing terms of the past. Some people find what is called 'political correctness' very irksome. That is partly because old habits of speech die hard, and partly because we still have a lot to learn about how to handle the new vocabulary. Most people, if they think about it, do not want to go back to the days of talking about 'lunatics' and 'cripples' and 'fallen women', and jeering at foreigners. All it is reasonable to ask is that we try to avoid labels which give offence to other people. The sort of language we use is important. If political correctness is handled sensibly, to avoid insulting or derogatory descriptions of groups whom we (as insiders) still tend to think of as outsiders, it is a powerful force for toleration. Some people will overdo it, and set verbal traps for the unwary, but that should not deter us from seeking a vocabulary that increases understanding and acceptance on the grounds of our common humanity. It is the lubrication that enables us to live together without grinding the wheels in conflict.

'God is not a Christian'

Desmond Tutu, former Archbishop of Cape Town, said in a sermon in Dublin in 2005, 'God is not a Christian',[19] adding that a purely Christian God 'would be a very small God'. That thought is startling, even shocking, to many people; but his meaning is that God created all humankind, and that Jesus Christ came to redeem all humankind, not to start a sect or denomination.

For the past 2,000 years, people have been trying to tie Jesus Christ down, to say that he supports this group or that group, to decide who's in and who's out; but the God who created and values all humankind cannot only be concerned with those who sport the right labels. Archbishop Rowan Williams has expressed the same thought in a subtle, many-layered analysis:

> The stranger . . . is neither the failed or stupid native speaker nor someone so terrifyingly alien that I cannot even tolerate the thought of learning from them. They represent the fact that I have growing to do, not necessarily into anything like an identity with them, but at least into a world where there may be more of a sense of its being a world we *share*.[20]

In another study, Archbishop Williams addresses the Other, and says:

> I must give up and put away all hopes of trapping you in my words, my categories and my ideas, my plans and my solutions. I shall offer you whatever I have to offer. I shall not commit the blasphemy (I don't use the word lightly) of ordering your life or writing your script.[21]

Such an open approach has its dangers. If we accept the Other (who, since globalization and mass population movements, is now living in our town, on our street, possibly next door), how are we to define our own identity? We are being forced to think about our own convictions, our own assumptions, our own prejudices. Rowan Williams writes in apparently limpid prose, but his words resonate. We must take the risk, in love. The basic Christian message is universal. The Holy Spirit is available for everybody, and can flow through some unexpected channels. It can operate in other faith groups as well as Christian ones. It can operate in 'secular' organizations. We cannot, in the modern world, see all activities labelled 'Christian' as 'the work of the Holy Spirit', and all activities carried out by other organizations as automatically less valid.

Do we live in a more secular world today? Perhaps it is only the labels that have changed. It was all so much easier when people lived where they were born, Sunday was a special day modelled on the Jewish Sabbath, and churchgoers wore their best hats. Some people think that society has fallen away sadly from Christian values and Christian standards; but we have to beware of what is called 'golden-age theory'. This is a social scientist's term for a sentimental harking back to a time when the Church was widely respected, everybody kept the Ten Commandments and lived as they should. This golden age never existed. Every society has its own golden-age theory – a belief in a time when life was simpler and values clearer: it is a very good example of functional myth. The ancient herdsmen who developed the story of Adam and Eve in primal innocence were indulging in golden-age theory; but human sin and human failure seem to be constant factors running right through history.

Does it matter that so many social welfare activities which were once managed by the Church are now controlled by central government or local authorities? Schools, hospitals and many forms of charitable activity began in a religious framework because that was the only form of social organization available to do the work, when the Church was the only agency to understand the need. Schools, hospitals, food kitchens, aid for travellers, help for those in poverty or suffering from disability were all set up on Christian initiatives, right from the early days of the Church.

Groups of Christians undertook this work because Jesus Christ told his disciples that they were to feed the hungry, give drink to the thirsty, welcome the stranger, clothe the naked, care for the sick, and visit the prisoner.[22] He said that anyone helping these despised and vulnerable people was directly helping him. We could scarcely have a clearer directive. The works of mercy were the test of real Christian belief. Only those who responded to the needs of others, loving their neighbours as themselves, were promised everlasting life. This was new thinking in the classical world, where human life came cheap. When Richard Dawkins feels wrenching compassion or charitable instincts, he is building on centuries of Christian capital. It is not likely that he would like the world without it.

Religious organizations handed much of this work over to public authorities, local, national and international, because it became too big for them. Major social programmes – insurance, employment, education, housing and others – demand the long-term planning, stable funding and advanced technical skills that only governments can provide. In the field of international voluntary social service, charity still has a link with its religious origins, indicated by such organizational titles as the Red Cross or Christian Aid. There is no shortage of national and local voluntary efforts – from the national charities and the sponsored programmes on television, such as *Comic Relief* or special editions of *Who Wants to be a Millionaire?*, to innumerable local initiatives. Where would we be without our church and Rotary groups, our sponsored runs, our flag days and our bazaars? In this respect, society as a whole has become more Christian, not less. The parable of the Good Samaritan still exerts a powerful influence; and the principle of working for the common good also applies to animal welfare, conservation, environmental care, disposing of noxious and toxic waste. It seems that we have only been given this one planet. We ought to take care of it.

Religion in a more tolerant world

At any state occasion in Britain with a religious presence (a royal wedding, a funeral, the consecration of an archbishop) we can expect to see in an Anglican cathedral the red cassock of a Roman Catholic cardinal, the blue-grey uniform of the Salvation Army, the tall hat of an Orthodox patriarch, the black of a Jewish rabbi, and even the yellow of a Buddhist monk's robe. Religious organizations are changing, too, and overcoming the hostilities and stereotypes of the past. If proximity brings friction, it can also bring understanding.

Richard Dawkins is strongly opposed to any kind of religious practice, ecumenical or not. He asks, 'Why do humans fast, kneel, genuflect, self-flagellate, nod maniacally towards a wall, crusade, or otherwise indulge in costly practices that can consume life and in extreme circumstances terminate it?'[23] This is a further example of his habit of throwing together quite disparate activities, and trying to tar them all with the same brush. Fasting, kneeling, genuflecting and bowing are common practices to indicate reverence in most religions, but not necessarily practised by all their adherents. Self-flagellation is a minority pursuit, and not one to be recommended. None of these activities is very expensive or life-threatening, and they have nothing to do with crusading or suicide bombing.

All religious practice is a stretching out to the divine. All the major religions are concerned with the power of the Infinite and the world we live in. They are all concerned with right behaviour. Most have rituals which include worship, cleansing with water, fasting, sharing food, going on pilgrimages to holy places, festivals associated with their founders like Christmas, the Passover, the birthday of the Prophet Muhammad or the birthday of the Buddha. Most have festivals associated with light and darkness, such as Candlemas, Diwali and the Chinese lantern festival. In all of them, there seem to be some worshippers who like chanting, candles, flowers, music and colourful ceremonies, and some who are drawn to plainer expressions of devotion; but why should Richard Dawkins object to how people worship merely on the grounds that he does not understand what they are doing, and therefore thinks their actions meaningless?

What the secular world calls tolerance, social cohesion, fellowship, positive emotions, respect for the rights of others is what Christians call the operation of the Holy Spirit. Wherever these features are found, the Holy Spirit is present; and when they are absent, no amount of prayer or invocation will produce it.

God created and cares for all human beings, Christian or not. In the twenty-first century, we have to learn to live with and share insights with the members of other faiths and other cultures, and work out a common system of human values. Christ's injunction, love God, and love your neighbour, is wide enough to cover all people of peace and good will, whatever religious label they choose.

That is enough to keep us busy for the next millennium at least. The Holy Spirit is still operating – blowing where it wills, a rushing wind, surprising us, upsetting our fixed ideas, prodding our sluggish minds into new patterns of thought. Sometimes the action of what Christians call the Lord and

Giver of Life is puzzling, and sometimes it is painful; but this dynamic force sweeps through our ageing social structures, promising us a new world when we are ready to live in it.

Key points

- The charges against religion listed in *The God Delusion* involve social, economic and political causes of conflict.
- Religious labels attached to opposing parties are often no more than labels, and conceal complex problems.
- Group loyalties and group hostilities are part of the fabric of social and political life.
- There has been a considerable advance in toleration and compassion in recent years. Richard Dawkins recognizes this, but is unable to account for it.
- A world without religion could not have produced this advance.
- Historically, the development of human rights comes from the Christian belief in the uniqueness of every human being. Christians regard it as the operation of the Holy Spirit.

8

What's Wrong with the World?

Everything is wrong with the world – war, suicide bombers, destruction, torture, sadism, perverted ideals and twisted thinking. Richard Dawkins feels that deeply, and attempts to blame religion for it all; but he does not point the accusing finger only at religious extremists. He says quite specifically, 'The take-home message is that we should blame religion itself, not religious extremism – as though that were some terrible perversion of real, decent religion.'[1] He says that there is no such thing as real, decent religion. Religious people are being unreal and anti-social in believing 'absurdities'.

Yet he does not maintain this extreme position when he examines real-life situations. He is less deterministic than some of his colleagues in the field of genetics. For example, Professor Steve Jones, the author of *In the Blood: Genes, God and Destiny*, argues that free will is nothing more than an illusion, because we are entirely conditioned by our genes. He suggests that although there may not be a 'criminal gene', the propensity to criminal behaviour is so established in some people that they should not be held responsible for their actions in law.[2] This view leaves no scope for moral choice; we act as our genes dictate. Richard Dawkins, on the other hand, believes that we should *teach* altruism. That implies that those who are taught are capable of learning. All the same, one can search his books in vain for mention of the great Christian themes – guilt, repentance, forgiveness. There is hardly any mention of them once he has disposed of Adam and Eve and the apple-scrumping. That he dismisses as a teenage prank.

Christians hold that human beings have free will, and can make moral choices. They are not zombies, and they are not monkeys. Our Creator could have made and kept us free from sin, but he gave us the freedom to choose, even the freedom to write books saying that he does not exist. That means that people are responsible for their own wrongdoing.

Free will and personal sin

Richard Dawkins is explosive about teaching on this subject. Clearly he thinks that Christians are a bunch of kill-joys. He says that early Christian theologians might have written 'extolling the sky splashed with stars, or mountains and green forests, seas and dawn choruses', but instead all they write about is 'sin sin sin sin sin sin sin.'[3] He evidently thinks that this subject is just the stock in trade of priests and other religious leaders.

Most people have a better understanding of wrongdoing than that – though many cast around, as he does, for someone else to blame. Some have knee-jerk reactions, and blame 'global capitalism', 'television', 'irresponsible parents' or 'politicians who don't listen' – targets as arbitrary as 'religion'; but people with a religious background are aware that acts have consequences, and that we must accept responsibility for what we do. We experience a sense of guilt – a conflict between our instincts and our moral sense. Kant dealt with the subject at length. It has preoccupied psychoanalysts since Freud and Jung, and dramatists and novelists for longer. Dostoievsky's *Crime and Punishment* would not have become a classic unless it resonated deep in the human psyche. The existentialist Jean-Paul Sartre complained bitterly about the burden of free will, writing of the individual 'condemned to be free', and thus put under intolerable pressure. There has always been this agonizing gap between how people behaved and how they knew they should behave. We cannot avoid wrongdoing, however hard we try. St Paul said, 'I do not do the good I want, but the evil I do not want is what I do.'[4]

The Ten Commandments are a list of 'don'ts' for an ancient people who had to be taught that way, as one teaches a child.[5] Jesus Christ summed them up in two positive commands: love the Lord your God with all your heart and all your soul and all your mind, and your neighbour as yourself. He told questioners, 'On these two commandments hang all the law and the prophets.'[6] A lawyer asked him to define what he meant by 'neighbour', and he told the story of the Good Samaritan: your neighbour is any human being in need, even a stranger and a foreigner.

The Seven Deadly Sins are a list of the kind of behaviour Christians are taught to avoid. The advertising world has long known that the quickest way to making a profit is to tempt people to commit one of them. Watch an evening's television, flip through the Sunday newspaper supplements, and see how openly the glossy advertisements appeal to Pride, Envy, Anger, Lust, Gluttony, Sloth and Avarice. We are encouraged to have the best house, the most impressive car, the latest fashion, the most trendy cooking, the softest bed, the most exotic holidays, the most exciting sex life. We are told to emulate 'seriously rich' people, and stun our neighbours with our success. It is often said that the deadly sin you forget is the one you are most likely to commit. The worst of all the deadly sins is Pride, which can lead people into committing the other six. Christians are told to begin with their own individual faults. *Mea culpa, mea culpa, mea maxima culpa.* This is not a philosophy congenial to a society which measures everything in terms of money.

Sin is often thought to be a matter of particular acts – stealing, murder, coveting and so on – in which we have a clear choice and make a deliberate decision; but we often act or fail to act because we do not understand a situation, or we did not think about the consequences, or because the people round us were doing the same thing. We are social beings, and our acts and choices have roots and contexts. In many human situations, we do not have stark alternatives of Sin and Good Behaviour. Perhaps that is what Richard Dawkins is trying to say when he rails against sin sin sin sin sin sin sin? Our actions occur in a network of cause and effect, and of interaction with other people. We are inclined to think of sin coming in parcels – big sins, small sins, more sin, less sin; but often sin is more like a dye poured into a mountain stream at source: it goes underground, disappearing for long periods, and then emerging to taint the water in unexpected places. In many tangled human problems, responsibility for what went wrong is very difficult to apportion. I am responsible for my own actions, but how far am I responsible for the actions of my family and my friends, or they for mine? Popular TV programmes like *Coronation Street* or *EastEnders* frequently deal with such issues – was it Sharon's fault or Darren's? Should Debbi have revealed that to Troy? Between identifiable Good and identifiable Evil there is an area of muddle and confusion, of not knowing what to do next, of realizing consequences too late, of good intentions going wrong; but all the same, sin is a fact of life. If you sleep around, cheat, lie, steal, drink too much, beat people up, your behaviour will have destructive effects on your own personality, and other people will suffer. Sexual acts outside a loving and long-term relationship destroy trust, and deny the real meaning of a sexual relationship. They may also result in the creation of a child – and children need loving and long-term relationships. They are not just renewed DNA.

Individual sin can be trivialized: sin is about much more serious things than mild indulgences like eating a few chocolates in Lent. It can be glamorized – for example, by advertisements; and it can be normalized. The portrayal on television of sex acts without affection; the publicity given to the lives of 'celebrities' who change partners as easily as they change their diets, the emphasis in so many plays and films on what the BBC euphemistically calls 'violence and strong language' all suggest that such behaviour is not only common, but acceptable. People have to learn to resist the pressures.

How are we to 'confess' and 'repent'? Jesus Christ cut through a maze of complexity by giving us the Lord's Prayer: we are to pray to be forgiven our sins in proportion to our capacity to forgive those who sin against us. That is a straight *quid pro quo*, simple to understand and devastatingly effective in puncturing self-righteousness. Repentance is not just the act of 'saying sorry'. It means identifying and regretting the wrong thing you did, making up for its ill effects as best you can, and being prepared to forgive other people for the wrongs done to you. It can be a long and complicated process: our sins are not washed away that easily. Saying 'I forgive you' is easy enough. The difficulty is meaning it, and keeping it up. Forgetting is even more difficult. If the other party is really trying to make amends, we can try. If the other party does not understand the nature of the wrong act, we can pray, like Christ on the cross, that they may be forgiven because they do not understand what they are doing.[7]

We are told to hate the sin and love the sinner; but there are circumstances in which that is very difficult. Suppose somebody knocks me down and steals my wallet, and while I lie there forgiving him, he kicks me in the ribs? A certain amount of indignation would be only human; but if loving the sinner is beyond our immediate capacity, we should at least try to understand what circumstances and pressures made him (or her) behave like that; if we get the opportunity, help him to understand what his actions do to other people. We should try to suffer the results quietly, because anger, even righteous anger, will destroy us; and we are told to judge not, then we will not be judged.

The natural reaction is to seek revenge. How many film titles begin with 'The Revenge of the . . . '? Revenge is an enormously popular theme in plays and novels. Jeffrey Archer made a fortune out of it in his first and very successful novel *Not a Penny More, Not a Penny Less*, published in 1975, the year before *The Selfish Gene*. There is great emotional satisfaction in setting the record straight, righting the wrong, rebalancing the scales of justice. 'He asked for it' or 'She got what she deserved' makes a good ending to a story.

Popular psychology tells us that repression is bad for us, but that is not the Christian response. Revenge is natural, but so are brute force, killing off the weak and cannibalism if you are hungry enough. Revenge is the philosophy of an eye for an eye and a tooth for a tooth. The response of forgiveness is 'unnatural' in that it is based not on natural instinct, but on an understanding of human nature and human failings. The important thing is not to retaliate.

Corporate sin

What are we to do when the whole of our society seems to be doing the wrong thing? How far are we individually responsible for what happens? Many of us are exercised about how to respond when we disagree with government action. We can march, we can write to the press, we can sign petitions, we can put a poster in the window saying 'Not in my name', we can make speeches; but like it or not, we are all implicated in the decisions made by our leaders – and more so in modern democracies than in imperial Rome.

What would Jesus Christ have done? He told us to love God and love our neighbours. In his time on earth, people did not have to contend with the kind of global movements that now seem to have developed a sinister life of their own. Would he have marched to ban the bomb, to defend human rights, to ban abortion or euthanasia? The Gospels of Matthew, Mark and Luke all quote him as saying that people should render unto Caesar the things that are Caesar's, and unto God the things that are God's – and individuals were left to decide which things came into which category. His appeal was always directly to the human heart, not to mass movements; but new methods of communication set us new problems.

Jesus Christ preached peace. We all want peace – or nearly all of us. Richard Dawkins wants peace. That 16-point list of his represents a revulsion against useless and needless suffering and mutilation. Like many of us, he has a general sense of powerlessness – of life getting out of control, of global forces nobody can handle, of politicians and public figures moving uncertainly through a maze of causes and consequences. So he blames religion. Does religion have any answers?

The Eastern religions face suffering with quiet resignation. The Dalai Lama, though he knows his way about the scientific world and is familiar with concepts like 'wave-particle duality', 'Schrödinger's cat' and 'paradigm shifts', preaches a remarkable gospel of peace and tranquillity in spite of persecution and exile.[8] Western religion is more proactive.

Conflict resolution

Religious leaders in South Africa have given the world an outstanding example of forgiveness that goes far beyond individual effort into the resolution of corporate evils. In the last years of the twentieth century, Nelson Mandela and Archbishop Desmond Tutu led the nation in the exercise of examining and cleansing the terrible wrongs of apartheid. The white vans of the Truth and Reconciliation Commission made their way across the veldt from township to township, and courts were set up like no other courts; for in these courts, there was no punishment and no recrimination as long as the accused told the whole truth.[9] Both white and black were encouraged to come forward, publicly admit their own guilt, and accept forgiveness. It was a long drawn-out exercise, and not very well reported by the British press, which had difficulty in understanding what was going on. Perhaps its effects were patchy; but the transfer of power in South Africa did not lead to the bloodbath many people had predicted, because revenge was stopped in its tracks.

The exercise has not received much publicity in Britain or the United States, but other countries are trying to use the same methods.[10] It is being repeated in the killing fields of Rwanda, in Liberia, Serbia and Montenegro. Georgia had a 'Velvet Revolution' without bloodshed, and this was followed by the 'Orange Revolution' in the Ukraine, and the 'Tulip Revolution' in Kyrgyzstan. Perhaps we are at last learning – in some places, some of the time – to go beyond naked aggression to reason and understanding.

Similarly, religious leaders have played a leading part in the attempts to bring peace and justice to Northern Ireland. Politicians from Gladstone to Bill Clinton and Tony Blair have toiled over the wrongs of the past. History has to be painfully undone; but this is another situation in which common sense and common humanity seem to be prevailing at last. The weapons of peace so often seem painfully inadequate when faced with the weapons of war, but change is possible, and we have seen it happen. Can the same sort of patient diplomacy solve the problems of Israel and the Palestinian territories, and other world trouble spots? If so, the outcome will depend on religious understanding, not on atheism.

Sickness and suffering

Even if the entire human race managed to live in a permanent state of absolute sanctity, if all the nations learned to repress their aggressive instincts and live together in perfect justice and amity, supported by first-class health services, people would still become old, grow ill and die. Our DNA wears out. Sickness and disability, ageing and death, are part of the human condition. Steve Jones puts this quite brutally:

> Every gene suffers the same fate . . . Sooner or later, the instructions become so garbled that bodily decay is an inexorable process . . . There may be more eighty-year-olds than there were, but there is still a notable shortage of those celebrating their one hundred and twentieth birthday.[11]

Our physical system is not designed to last. We can rush off to the gym, the hairdresser, the beauty salon or the plastic surgeon at the sight of the first extra pound in weight, the first grey hair, the first wrinkle, but nothing stops the process for long. This is what it means to be human: we are born, we grow up, we age, and eventually we die. Steve Jones believes that our only hope of immortality is through sex, which renews the ageing genes to form a new human being in whom the process of ageing and decay will start all over again.

This, of course, is where we started in Chapter 1: with Richard Dawkins' belief that individuals are 'fleeting things' and genes, like diamonds, are for ever. Genetics can tell us no more than this; but religion has some answers. Jesus Christ healed sick people – blind, deaf and dumb, paraplegic, demented and lepers. Christians, Jews, Hindus, Buddhists and people of other faiths all practise healing. Flesh decays. It is perishable stuff; and many doctors and nurses must have wondered why we were not made of something less easily damaged.

Just a minute: do we really want to live down here for ever, getting older and older, and rushing off to the gym when we are 120? Look at the physical world: the plants push through the earth, bud, flower, fruit and die, lie fallow in winter and wait for the spring, when the whole process starts again. There is a built-in system of renewal. Whatever the purpose is, this dying and re-growth is part of it.

Does that explain pain and suffering? Not really. It does not explain why there are malformed babies, children scream-ing with meningitis, young people with cancer and heart conditions, old people with vacant minds in decaying bodies.

In the ancient world, and through much of the Middle Ages, most people took it for granted that pain and suffering were divinely inflicted as a punishment for sin. The assump-tion that only wicked people suffered made it easier to put up with other people's suffering, if not one's own. Sodom and Gomorrah were wiped off the map. Good people prospered, bad people came to a satisfyingly unpleasant end; but we see too many good people suffer, and too many bad people prosper, to believe that. True, suffering can sometimes be a learning process. It can strip away all the daily preoccupa-tions and assumptions, and bring one up against the basic facts of human existence. Some people become gentler, kinder and more open to spiritual development as a result, but others become querulous, demanding and full of self-pity. Some are very frightened. Some spend all their time fighting the pain. Some curse God for inventing it. In a hospice, one can see all these reactions in people in the final stages of life. The basic principle of the hospice movement is to help patients to find a better quality of life in what time is left to them.

Suffering in children is particularly hard to understand because it seems both cruel and purposeless. Small children do not understand what is happening to them, or have the resources to deal with pain and uncertainty. Perhaps such situations were more easily dealt with in Victorian times, when families were large, and most parents lost a child or two. Today, medical advances have made it possible to save many children's lives, but families are much smaller and expectations have risen. When a child has a terminal illness, we are appallingly conscious of the pain and the loss and the waste.

Cruelty in the natural world

If we turn to animal life, we find the same evidence of cruelty and suffering. Cats catch mice, eagles catch fish and birds, lions and tigers in the wild kill and eat deer and zebra, and a dead or dying lion will attract a host of smaller hungry predators. Nature is permanently, horribly carnivorous. Richard Dawkins knows this, and it troubles him. In *A Devil's Chaplain*, he describes the universe as clumsy, wasteful and blundering. Though he teaches the principle of natural selection, it appals him because it is cruel.[12] He is grieved by the death of the elegant racing gazelle. Perhaps he saw one die as a child in Kenya. There are actually much nastier places in the world than the East African savannah. What would the child Richard have made of the Everglades of Florida, where alligators crawl along the banks, and birds of prey sit on rotting branches waiting for something to die? There is a particularly nasty one called the *anhinga*, or snake-bird. What would he have made of the rainforests of Borneo or Brazil, where red or white ants can make very short work of a carcase or even a living person unable to move? What would he have made of the arid deserts where the bones of long-dead camels bleach in the unbearable sun?

Nature is not all pretty. Even the most fervent nature-lover has to deal with William Blake's question about the tiger: 'Did he who made the lamb make thee?' If God made intricate and delightful things like ladybirds and butterflies and toucans, he also made slugs and snakes and scorpions. Biologists assure us that they have their place in the evolutionary chain. Victor Hugo said, 'La Nature est une grande roue que ne mouve pas sans écraser quelqu'un' (Nature is a great wheel which cannot move without crushing something). Or someone.

Natural disasters

The case against God seems to be building up. What about natural disasters? When the tsunami hit South-East Asia, when the earthquakes killed thousands of people on the borders between Kashmir and Pakistan, when the hurricane devastated New Orleans, who else was to blame? How can we believe in a God who is not only clumsy, wasteful and callous, but kills off innocent people by the thousand?

Many thoughtful people have been turned away from faith by the sheer horrors of which the universe seems capable, quite apart from the horrors which humankind inflicts upon it; but the two are not entirely separate. Many natural disasters are made much worse by human action. The effects of the tsunami in South-East Asia are thought to have been made much worse by the removal of natural barriers – sand dunes and coral reefs – to make coastal districts more attractive to tourists. The new hotels needed rooms with a sea view, and safe off-shore cruises. The tsunami was followed by looting, corpse-robbing and the seizure of young children to be sold into slavery. The impact of Hurricane Katrina in New Orleans would have been much less dreadful if the levees had been properly constructed and if the authorities had had an effective emergency plan for the thousands – mainly poor, mainly black – who were left stranded. They were left without food or water, helplessly waving from rooftops while helicopters circled overhead, and journalists and photographers did nothing to help them.

That shamed the United States. Whenever there is a disaster, someone profits. Famine in Africa is made much worse by corrupt politicians, heavy burdens of debt to the World Bank, and trade barriers. Help for earthquake victims in Kashmir has to wait while border disputes flare between India and Pakistan. Every disaster brings tales of bravery and self-sacrifice – but it also brings stories of human greed and incompetence.

So human beings have to take some of the blame – but not all. Whatever action we take, however generous our giving, however efficient our rapid-response services, the basic causes of such disasters are beyond our control. After the tsunami, there was a lively correspondence in the press on the lines of 'Whose fault is it?' The Archbishop of Canterbury, when asked, said honestly that the cause was a mystery to him, but that it was up to us to deal with the consequences. Some correspondents said that the disaster had brought them closer to God. Others said that it had led them to reject the idea of God altogether. A geologist brought the discussion to a close by pointing out that earthquakes were essential to the evolution of our planet. If there were no earthquakes, there would be no mountain ranges. The entire earth would be flat and covered with water, and human life would never have developed. This ball of fire on whose thin crust we live is constantly changing and evolving, and much of what it does is hostile to humankind. Seismologists and oceanographers struggle to predict what it is going to do next. In California, the San Andreas fault is a threat to communities all along the Pacific coast. Even in relatively stable Western Europe, rivers change course, and coastlines are constantly silting up or being eroded.

The Christian analysis

What can our Creator be like if he not only allows disasters to happen, but actually creates the conditions that make them occur? The problem is a very old one. St Paul knew about it, and took it seriously. 'We know', he wrote to the Church in Galatia, 'that the whole creation has been groaning in labour pains until now.'[13] That is a modern translation, and a curious one, for the earth is old and steeped in wrongdoing, not giving birth. Actually St Paul did not mention labour pains. The Greek New Testament makes it plain that the original version was simply that the whole creation groaned together. There are other reasons for groaning.

What St Paul says quite clearly is that Jesus Christ came to bring about a new creation. The old creation was 'subject to futility by the will of the one who subjected it'. This sounds as though he is saying that God made everything go wrong on purpose – the passage is a difficult one, much debated by theologians; but it makes sense in the context of the whole passage in his letter to the Romans. He tells them that 'the sufferings of the present time' are necessary because of the glory that is to come. He goes on to talk about hope, and how they must wait with patience for the new revelation.

St Paul, like the apostles, probably expected the Second Coming to be almost immediate. It seems reasonable to point out that here we are, nearly 2,000 years later, still struggling and suffering and hoping. If God created a world capable of corruption in which we are all born to groan and travail, it seems that he has kept us waiting for a very long time.

But in fact, none of us has been kept waiting for 2,000

years. We do not live that long. Our groaning and travailling lasts only a few decades. All the same, it is not unreasonable to ask, 'Is it worth it?' Is St Paul being unduly optimistic in believing that there is a purpose to it all? Cosmologists talk about 'design flaws' in the universe, as if it were a new car or a fresh version of Word. That sounds like a more rational explanation, the sort of explanation that fits our own experience; but where do we go from there?

If there are design flaws, there must be a design, and a Designer. Any scientist who thinks he can identify design flaws must think that (with the aid, presumably, of a celestial computer), he could have made a better job of it; but the Creator of the universe surely cannot be incompetent. We have enough evidence of 'fine-tuning' to trust that he has got it right. If God could get the pull of gravity and the mix of the air we breathe exactly right, why should he make elementary mistakes about tectonic plates?

If earthquakes and physical decay are part of the design, just what is the design, how good is it, and how big is it? We simply do not know. Richard Dawkins thinks that there are 'wonders' beyond our grasp, but when the same problems are put into theological language, he talks of 'rubbish' and 'absurdities', and thunders against mystery. Because he cannot confront God and argue with him, he assumes that God does not exist. He quotes Bertrand Russell, 'No evidence, God; no evidence.' In *The Blind Watchmaker*, he comes very close to challenging God directly. He says that the ultimate atheist's test would be to challenge God to strike him by lightning. He estimates (or possibly works out on his computer) that the chances of actually being struck by lightning at the moment when he said the words would be about half a million to one against;[14] but he is a cautious man. A careful reader will note that he never actually issues the challenge.

A cosmic problem?

The whole of human life is concerned with morality, with the battle between our selfish instincts and our consciences. We know from the earthly life of Jesus Christ that he was prepared to bring the message of what Richard Dawkins calls 'altruism' – loving your neighbour, helping the stranger – at appalling cost to himself: the cost of living as a human being, and letting other human beings do their worst to him. God in action came into the world, and the world came into being through him, yet the world did not know him.[15] Do the causes of our distress lie beyond the world we know – even beyond those parts of the universe which we can observe with our most sophisticated equipment? Super-telescopes will give us some idea of its immensity, but they will not tell us what it is for.

The twenty-first century does not like extraterrestrial explanations unless they come in the form of science fiction or fantasy. They belong to the category known to the book trade as 'sword and sorcery'; but it is remarkable how popular these stories are in our otherwise prosaic age. In the 1950s, J. R. R. Tolkien and C. S. Lewis, who were friends and colleagues, recognized that this genre of writing appealed to many people who would never dream of reading a theological text. They decided that the best way of getting their message across was to write their tentative explanations of the universe in fictional form. Tolkien, who was a Roman Catholic, based his *Lord of the Rings* cycle on the ancient Nordic myths. Lewis, who was an Anglican, based his *Cosmic Trilogy*[16] on science fiction. These were parallel attempts – the first in time and the second in space – to think beyond the limits of everyday experience.

Both told an epic story of discovery, adventure, hostility, battles against dark forces, danger, failure, redemption and ultimate victory. Each found a way through allegory of telling the cosmic story – what the universe was all about: they did not explain sin away, or attribute it all to human misdemeanours. They thought that the force of evil was real and powerful, capable of taking many shapes and speaking through many people.

In the last book in the New Testament, the Revelation of St John the Divine, we can find the source of their inspiration. The writer describes a remarkable vision of the extraterrestrial origin of evil. War breaks out in heaven, and St Michael and the angels battle against 'that ancient serpent who is called the Devil and satan, the deceiver of the whole world'.[17] This is what theologians term the doctrine of the Pre-Mundane Fall, the introduction of evil before the creation of the world, as opposed to the Post-Mundane Fall, occasioned by the original sin of Adam and Eve. Satan corrupts the Earth, including the world of men and women, the animal world, the world of nature, and the very stuff of which the planet is made – and the battle still rages.

Richard Dawkins calls the book of the Revelation 'one of the weirdest books in the Bible'.[18] It is so much at odds with the factual material of the rest of the New Testament – the records, travel diaries and letters – that it was nearly left out. The commentary in the Jerusalem Bible calls it an allegory, and notes that it has a distinct literary form. It belongs to the apocalyptic writing common in Jewish circles in the early Christian era, and probably dates from about the year 96. J. B. Phillips' translation from the Greek[19] treats it as the vision of a very old man, sometimes almost incoherent with the effort of conveying the burning images in his mind. He sees a new heaven and a new earth, where all our trials and sufferings make sense at last.

Our understanding is blocked by the limitations of our five senses; by the space–time continuum. We are Aquinas's bats blinking in the sun, or ape-descendants straining our eyes to see distant horizons if Richard Dawkins prefers. It all adds up to the same thing: a universe of wonders which are beyond our capacity to grasp. We can only deal with these great questions in allegory, but we do have advantages over the African apes. We can analyse our own behaviour, we can use complex language, we can understand the nature of moral problems; and we can ask questions. In Karl Popper's terms, we are problem-solving creatures. We will keep on framing the questions, trying out solutions, identifying errors, redefining the questions and trying again.

$$P_1 \dashrightarrow TS \dashrightarrow EE \dashrightarrow P_2 \,..$$

This procedure is not only basic to scientific investigation. It applies to every field of human enquiry. Curiosity is our defining characteristic. We are constantly discovering new horizons and new problems. In the past 60 or 70 years, we have plucked a whole basket of fresh apples from the Tree of Knowledge: nuclear fission, satellite communication, new discoveries about gender and human sexuality, organ transplants, stem-cell research and many more. Some of our discoveries are beneficial. Some are confusing and puzzling. Some are frankly terrifying – including the knowledge of what we are doing to our precious little planet. We are being given new knowledge, and being told to learn how to deal with it.

Is our moral understanding keeping pace with our scientific achievements? Many people are concerned that it is not. Though God may not play dice, there are times when he seems to be playing for very high stakes; but if we have free will, we have to be free to make mistakes. When a child learns arithmetic, there has to be the possibility of getting the sums wrong. If all the answers were always right, the child would not be learning at all. If an artist wants to paint in oils, it has to be possible to get the colours wrong, or to paint a line in the wrong place, otherwise the result would only be painting by numbers. There is simply no way, even for God himself, of giving freedom and at the same time controlling the outcome.

The power of reason and the development of knowledge take us much further today than in earlier centuries, but there is still a point where, as philosophers as diverse as St Paul, Thomas Aquinas and Kant have explained so powerfully, reason cannot take us all the way to full understanding. When we come up against that blank wall, we all become Thomas's blinking bat, facing the blaze of the sun. Richard Dawkins, with his talk of African apes and limited vision and burkas, is expressing something very similar – though he thinks that only science can get us through the barrier.

Christians believe that God suffers in our suffering. In the third century, there was a school of thought called the Patripassian heresy which held that God felt all human and animal pain. Tertullian, the Carthaginian theologian, wrote about it. In the twelfth century, Peter Abelard and the schoolmen of Paris knew about it. It was rejected then because people were thinking in terms of earthly time, and not of eternity. If God is omniscient and compassionate, he must know what he is putting us through. He must have *experienced* it. The only bit of that experience which we can see in human history is Christ's suffering on Calvary; but St Paul told us that we see in a glass darkly (or in a mirror dimly in the modern versions), and that faith and hope will lead us through the confusion to clarity.

The fear and the horror only seem to make sense if this life is a trial run, and the real life starts when it is over. God's great experiment must involve another world – or worlds – beyond this one. If this is reality, only the physical body dies, and all our struggles and sorrows are not the ultimate tragedy they seem. What nineteenth-century scientists dismissed as theological fantasy becomes increasingly possible as we explore the universe and the stuff of which it is made. Discoveries like shadow matter, dark energy and the possibility of parallel universes take us far beyond the 'real world' of common understanding.

Unless there is another life to come, this life is as meaningless and without purpose as Richard Dawkins would have us believe, no more than a sick joke. For each of us, there comes a time when we will have to stop arguing about whether we 'believe in God' or not. We shall be faced with ultimate reality; but we were born to question. The answers may have to wait until we are ready for them.

Key points

- The physical sciences offer no clues to two of the major problems of human existence: the existence of sustained and violent conflict, and the process of ageing and death.
- In the field of religion, the doctrine of sin and forgiveness offers a means of dealing with wrong behaviour. Religious insights are increasingly being used on a national and international scale as a means of conflict resolution.
- The problem of suffering runs right through the natural world. Child suffering, animal suffering and the suffering of thousands in natural disasters are particularly hard to explain.
- The Christian answer is that God suffers, too. Suffering is the corollary of free will – perhaps on a cosmic scale. Most people can only deal with these ideas in allegory. Myth and science fiction have been a means of disseminating them to a wider public.
- Neither scientists nor theologians know all the answers;

but the religious belief that the human spirit survives the destruction of DNA is strengthened rather than weakened by recent scientific discoveries.

9

Next

There is not much about death in *The God Delusion*. Richard Dawkins has that atheist line about facing ultimate annihilation unafraid, and standing tall to face the far horizon; but as so often, when there is a subject that he does not want to deal with, he trivializes it. He starts from A. A. Milne's *Now We Are Six*, with Binker, Christopher Robin's imaginary friend, who is 'always there'.[1] We get nearly a whole page of Binker, followed by some reminiscences on how he, Richard Dawkins, used to imagine that he was a little boy pretending to be Richard, and a discussion on whether ancestral gods are Binker-substitutes or Binkers are ancestral god-substitutes. This looks very like displacement. Death is a grown-up subject, and he is not facing it here at a grown-up level.

There are a few more mature comments from his favourite authors. Thomas Jefferson makes a reappearance. Jefferson wrote to friends in his last days saying that he had neither fear of death nor hope of a future life. Mark Twain wrote: 'I do not fear death. I had been dead for billions and billions of years before I was born, and had not suffered the slightest inconvenience from it.' Bertrand Russell is even more bracing: 'Even if the open windows of science at first make us shiver after the cosy indoor warmth of traditional humanising myths, the fresh air brings vigour, and the great spaces have a splendour of their own.' Richard Dawkins calls this 'strong meat',[2] but the comment is somewhat obscure. If death is the absolute end, there is no prospect of either fresh air or great spaces, splendid or otherwise. Richard Dawkins might have quoted his other favourite author, Woody Allen, who said, 'I'm not afraid of death. I just don't want to be there when it happens'; but perhaps that is too near the bone.

The death of Douglas Adams

He thinks much more seriously about death and dying in *A Devil's Chaplain*. He writes: 'One of the signs of growing older is that one ceases to be invited to be best man at weddings or godfather at christenings. I have just begun to write obituaries, speak eulogies and organise funerals.'[3] He was 60 years old when he wrote that. He includes in that book several pieces of writing about friends who have died, and a long account of his reaction to the death of Douglas Adams.[4]

He was not present when Douglas Adams died. He was in England, and Douglas Adams died in California. He describes how at ten past seven in the morning, he 'shuffled out of bed and looked at the e-mail' and found a message that told him the news. Douglas Adams, only 49 years old and apparently fit, had died from a sudden and unexpected heart attack, in the gym. Richard Dawkins' first reaction was 'Douglas, you cannot be dead'. He was probably only half awake when he switched on the e-mail. His friendship with Douglas Adams was largely conducted by e-mail. Wherever the two of them were in the world, the ideas, the jokes, the wild speculations flew back and forth from one to the other. Now there would be no more e-mails. He wondered whether he should wake his wife and tell her the news. She had known Douglas Adams longer than he had – they worked together on the script of *Dr Who*. He decided that it was too early, so he sat down immediately and wrote his 'Lament for Douglas' for the *Guardian*. In it, he says that he simply could not believe the news. It was 'the classic double-take'. Then 'that other cliché, the words swelling before my eyes . . . It must be part of the joke. It must be some other Douglas Adams.' He had lost 'an irreplaceable intellectual companion, and one of the kindest and funniest men I ever met'. He tried to think 'The sun is shining, life must go on, seize the day and all those clichés.'

He determined to go out that same day and buy a tree, a Douglas fir, 'tall upright, evergreen', and plant it in memory of his tall friend, who was 'nearer seven foot than six'. Before he sent off the 'Lament', he added a note to say that the tree had been bought and planted. 'Was it cathartic?' he asks himself, and replies, 'No, but it was worth a try.'[5]

This account carries a genuine sense of loss. His first reaction was incredulity, followed by the 'Stop All the Clocks' feeling.[6] Time's arrow points in only one direction. His close friend and colleague had disappeared through a hole in the world's fabric, and yet the sun was still shining, life was going on. After that, he needed a ritual, and he devised one of his own – the Douglas fir, the lament for the *Guardian*, and later the tribute at St Martin-in-the-Fields.

He evidently went on grieving. Five years after Douglas Adams' death, in *The God Delusion,* he wrote: 'Douglas, I miss you. You are my cleverest, funniest, most open-minded, wittiest, tallest and possibly only convert. I hope this book might have made you laugh – though not as much as you made me.'[7]

A Devil's Chaplain also includes two other obituaries, both written for atheists. One is for Dr W. D. Hamilton, another evolutionist and Fellow of New College, Oxford – a delightful eccentric by all accounts. The other was for the journalist John Diamond, who met death with remarkable courage. Diamond had cancer of the throat. He charted his own gradual decline, and communicated it to other people through articles in the *Sunday Times*. When Richard Dawkins met him, he was unable to speak, but he 'carried on lively and cheerful conversations by writing in a notebook'. One of the emotions that fuelled John Diamond through the last stages was anger against the exaggerated claims made for alternative medicine, often for profit. Diamond wrote a book called *Snake Oil and Other Preoccupations*, and after he died Richard Dawkins wrote a foreword to it praising his intellectual courage and his refusal to accept 'the security blanket of irrational superstition'.[8] He admires John Diamond for going out 'with guns blazing'. Many people are too ill and too confused to think very clearly about anything when they reach the final stage, but John Diamond was not. His mind was clear, and he stared death in the face.

Richard Dawkins knows that this bleak philosophy, which he shares, has nothing to offer to 'the dying patients, the weeping bereaved, the lonely Eleanor Rigbys for whom God is their only friend'.[9] He may feel 'wrenching compassion', but he says 'religion's power to console doesn't make it true'.

That is fair enough, but there is another of his tricks in the argument: what he does *not* say is that religion's power to console does not make it false, either. He writes as though the fact that religion consoles the lonely Eleanor Rigbys (of the Beatles' song) is evidence that it must be untrue, and of course it is nothing of the kind. It is impossible to prove a negative. The question of whether religion is true is not affected by whether it is comforting or not.

Final answers

Who really knows what happens after death? Nobody. Not the Archbishop of Canterbury; not the Pope; not the Moderator of the Free Church Council; not the Chief Rabbi; not the Ayatollahs; not the Dalai Lama. Christian theologians who specialize in eschatology (the study of the Four Last Things: death, judgement, heaven and hell) can only point to clues in the Bible.

The Eastern religions have a variety of theories about reincarnation and eventual assimilation into the One. Sufis – Islamic mystics – and some Hindus and Buddhists write of the soul being absorbed in the divine as the raindrop is absorbed in the ocean. The Chinese, a pragmatic people, do not appear given to speculation. Writers like Chuang Szu and Confucius speak of 'heaven' as the place of perfect justice and right living, but do not attempt to describe it, or to say how Righteous Man is to get there.[10]

None of us knows for certain, because we are all still alive, and the seal between this world and the next seems complete.

It is very mysterious. We are born into circumstances over which we have no control. We follow a path with many forks in it where we have to make repeated choices, many of which we do not fully understand until long after we have made them. We are eventually taken out of the world without our consent, at a time not of our choosing, to circumstances of which we know almost nothing; but religious belief includes an explanation for this, and atheism does not. If we had a cast-iron guarantee that we would survive the death of the body and face our Creator, what would happen to free will and the power of moral choice? We would be forced into good behaviour. We would have no option.

Dying

Woody Allen was right. What most people fear is less being dead than the process of dying. We cannot program a natural death. Some people, like Douglas Adams, die very quickly. Some 'make a good death' over months or even years, believing that there is another life ahead of them, and co-operating in the process of getting beyond the physical body. Some die violently. Some resist right up to the end.

Death smoothes out any fear or pain in that blank expression that nurses and undertakers often call 'peaceful'; but we know that the person has gone, and only the physical shell is left. The vital spirit – what Richard Dawkins calls 'the power' – has gone. He thinks that Douglas Adams just stopped happening. All that passion for living, all that irreverent humour, all that knowledge, just stopped. What do doctors and nurses and relatives say when somebody dies? They say 'He's gone' or 'She's gone', automatically, perhaps without thinking. They know that what is left is not a person, but just something to be tidied away.

Richard Dawkins is a strong supporter of euthanasia. He says, 'The process of dying could be, depending on our luck, painful and unpleasant.' He thinks it reasonable to avoid all that – the loss of capacity, the pain, the reliance on other people, the sense of helplessness. 'When I am dying, I should like my life to be taken out under a general anaesthetic, exactly as if it were a diseased appendix.'[11]

Does he mean this? Probably; but unless one is in very great pain, it must take a lot of cold courage; and by the time one is in very great pain, it is often too late to travel to the places where euthanasia is legal. In Britain, it is illegal. There are hard cases in which people linger on in pain, and that is very distressing to watch; but there are very real social dangers in legalizing euthanasia. The death of one person is often very convenient to others – their heirs, for example, or hard-pressed relatives. If euthanasia was legal and commonly available, there could be discreet – or not so discreet – pressure to encourage very vulnerable people to accept it. This is a particular threat as the expectation of life increases. In P. D. James' sombre novel, *The Children of Men*, the aged and helpless are taken away with many comforting reassurances about their future well-being, and then quietly drowned. This is one of those moral slippery slopes, and we do well to avoid it. Medical practitioners are taught to preserve life as long as possible. Most civilized countries find capital punishment unacceptable. We are all horrified by murder. People will fight for their own survival in the most extreme conditions. Life is precious.

'*Timor mortis conturbat me*' wrote the Tudor poet William Dunbar: the fear of death confuses me. He had faith that Christ had risen from the tomb and defeated death, but he knew that death was serious and puzzling. Christ himself feared death in Gethsemane. To avoid death, to avoid thinking about it, is a normal human reaction.

We know that death can be ugly, and we have an instinct to tidy it up. Close the eyes, draw up the sheet, fold the hands, wash the body. Perhaps it is meant to be ugly, so that we wait our turn. The urge to preserve life is so common, and so instinctive, that it seems to be functional: that this is the way we are programmed to react, so that we have the courage to go on living.

Though most people resist talking seriously about death, shying away from the subject and shrugging it off, not many turn to childish humour. A psychoanalyst might find Richard Dawkins' retreat to Binker significant.

Watching death on television is different. Murder mysteries are comfortable viewing, because we know that the man on the floor is covered with tomato sauce and not really dead, even if his eyes are open; or when TV archaeologists dig up somebody's lawn and brandish grinning skulls, because the

owners of the skulls died centuries ago, so we know nothing about them, and need not feel for them; or even when the
bodies of tsunami victims are shown on the news programmes
– provided that they are laid out neatly in rows and suitably
shrouded. They are strangers and foreigners on the other side
of the world. The newsreader will warn the audience if pictures
are likely to be 'distressing', so that the susceptible can look
away. Television shields us from the bite of real experience.

Funerals

The Victorians used to celebrate funerals with great pomp
and ceremony: black-plumed horses, black-bordered hand-
kerchiefs, long periods of mourning, and statues of weeping
angels in the cemetery. It was called 'paying respect', and very
poor people used to pay the insurance man a penny a week to
make sure that they had 'a proper funeral'. The outward show
was good for the funeral industry, and the procedure enabled
people to cloak their emotions in what was then regarded as a
decent manner by clinging to a ritual. Today, in a less devout
but more honest society, there is a strong reaction against the
Victorian Way of Death.

Richard Dawkins thinks that 'all funerals are sad, but secular funerals properly organised are preferable on all counts'.[12]
He likes 'the memoirs, the poems, the music', 'well-crafted
speeches' rather than 'hollow prayers'. He does not find the
words of the service helpful. How could he, when he thinks
they are unbelievable? He may be dogmatic, arrogant and self-
opinionated, but he is not a hypocrite. People who do believe
them often value the support of prayers that have sustained
many earlier generations through the experience of sorrow
and loss, though some now prefer to compose their own
service in order to commemorate a life rather than focusing
on the event of death.

Many people find it difficult to concentrate at funerals. There is an air of unreality. The only comfort is in the presence of other living people, and the thought that it is not our turn – yet; though we are very conscious that eventually the bell tolls for us all. We find it hard to imagine that someone we know and love can possibly be in that box, about to be put into that hole; and the words of the service, 'The Lord gave, and the Lord has taken away', can slip past our ears without meaning. To say 'I would rather remember him when he was alive' is a normal human reaction. We knew a living person, and what is being committed to the ground (or to the fire in cremation) is only something which that living person has left behind. So we leave the cemetery, and there is a great sense of relief when we can busy ourselves passing round the cups of tea or the drinks, and talk about something ordinary – mortgages, football, the children, anything.

This gap between what we are expected to experience at funerals and how we actually feel when we attend one is what psychologists call 'cognitive dissonance'. It is very common, and seems to be instinctive. We seem to be programmed to live, not to stay with the dead.

Memorials

Books on 'grieving' – there are many of them these days – usually tell the reader that it is normal to grieve for about three months. After that, we should 'seek closure' and look for a way forward; but it is not always that easy. There is no real closure after the death of someone whose life has touched our own, this side of our own death. That is the price of caring.

Richard Dawkins' memorial for Douglas Adams was a tree – a living organism that could anchor its roots in the earth and grow tall like the man it symbolized. That solution met both his enduring grief and his conviction that what happens to the earthly body was unimportant. Whether by burial or cremation, the body returns to the earth and breaks into its constituent atoms.

Some people still seem to find comfort in elaborate memorials, others react against this kind of remembrance. The poem that begins 'Do not stand at my grave and weep, I am not there, I do not sleep' is often recited at funerals, and it expresses a popular reaction. It goes on:

> I am a thousand winds that blow,
> I am the diamond glints on snow,
> I am the sun on ripened grain,
> I am the gentle autumn rain . . .
> Do not stand at my grave and cry,
> I am not there, I did not die.

When it was read on a British television programme in 1995, there were more than 30,000 requests for copies. A year later, it was voted 'the Nation's Favourite Poem' on a *Bookworm* poll. Nobody knew who wrote it. After much cross-Atlantic enquiry, it was found to be the work of an American housewife, Mary E. Frye, who died in 2004 at the age of 98. She never published it herself, and so did not own the copyright. It is a powerful assertion of the continuation of life and the vitality of the universe. The writer sees her own death as returning to the earth, and tells her friends that they will find her in the growing corn, the wind and the snow. That is a gentle thought, but the Christian faith offers us more. It claims that we survive as personalities, and do not go whirling round the earth as unidentifiable atoms.

After death

'In him was life, and the life was the light of all people,' writes St John. Christ told his disciples, 'Behold, I go to prepare a place for you', and, 'In my Father's house are many dwelling-places.'[13] The older versions of the Bible say 'mansions', but apparently mansions are no longer thought appropriate in this democratic age. Whether the dwelling-places are houses, flats or palaces, they must house people of many diverse views, including some who stoutly maintain that they are atheists, because they cannot bear the cruelty and injustice of the world, and blame God for it.

A note in *The God Delusion* suggests that Richard Dawkins has read his way through the Philip Pullman novels, but he does not seem tempted to go down that particular road of New Age pick-and-mix.[14] He is strongly opposed to any concept of life after death, and the main target of his attack is the Roman Catholic doctrine of purgatory. In Roman Catholic theology, purgatory is the place to which those who die in a state of grace go to expiate their unforgiven sins before being finally admitted to the Beatific Vision. Many people find it natural to pray for their dead friends and relatives, because they feel still attached to them, and perhaps because they sense that they have more learning to do after death. At its most merciful, the doctrine of purgatory allows for people to go on growing in the next life; but it has been the source of much superstition and abuse in the past, coupled with some sadistic ideas about punishment and retribution. Richard Dawkins describes purgatory as

> a sort of divine Ellis Island, a Hadean waiting room where the dead souls go if their sins aren't bad enough to send them to hell, but they still need a bit of remedial checking out and purifying before they can be admitted to the sin-free zone of heaven.[15]

This is a comparatively mild description of the doctrine of purgatory. In Cardinal Newman's poem, *The Dream of Gerontius*, we are given a much more terrifying account. People who know it through Elgar's superb music do not always pay much attention to the theology. Newman wrote it in 1865, 20 years after he left the Church of England to become a Roman Catholic.[16] It tells the story of an old man who dies in great pain. He goes to purgatory, where he endures more suffering for the good of his soul, and eventually an angel takes him to see the Beatific Vision; but he is so conscious of his own sins, and so blinded by glory, that he flees from the Vision, and rushes back into purgatory. This is a dreadful picture. Had the old man not suffered enough? What was the angel thinking of, taking him up to heaven before he was ready? How could a compassionate God just let him run away?

Many people believe in the Day of Judgement, and this doctrine has similarly given rise to awe and terror. It has inspired many great artists. Michaelangelo, Raphael, Titian and all the masters of the Renaissance depicted it on canvas or in fresco. Hieronymus Bosch's nightmare visions concentrated on hell, with much attention to the temptations and torments of the damned. Dante worked out the themes of heaven and hell in great detail in his *Paradiso* and *Inferno*. Perhaps we are moving towards a better understanding of God as we move to a more caring view of fatherhood. There is something to be said for Stanley Spencer's 1920s vision of the resurrection – the Cookham villagers climbing stolidly out of their graves in their unfashionable, crumpled clothes, gently encouraged by angels. A splendid version of the York Mystery Plays some years ago presented a much more active and compassionate view of Christ, played by the actor Art Malik. This Christ did not sit aloof in judgement. He strode about energetically, careless of his crown and his golden robe, pulling people out of dark holes where the flames flickered, and helping them up the ladder to heaven. God cares for people: he does not terrify people into accepting him.

St Paul had some remarkable things to say about the next life. In his first letter to the Corinthians, he tells them that *bios*, physical life, dies, but *zoe*, spiritual life, survives. He says:

> Listen, I will tell you a mystery! We will not all die, but we will be changed in a moment, in the twinkling of an eye, at the last trumpet. For the trumpet will sound, and the dead will be raised imperishable, and we will be changed.[17]

The Christian message that we will be changed and raised is clear enough; but much of our thinking about the afterlife (even St Paul's thinking) is limited by terrestrial concepts. We imagine the dead *waiting* in their graves for the Day of Judgement, or *spending time* in a place called purgatory where the prayers of the living can mitigate their sufferings; but the dead are beyond earthly time and space, in eternity, a state beyond our understanding. All we can do is to remember them with love, and celebrate the rites of passage.

Rites of passage are ways of celebrating and marking steps from one stage of life to the next. We celebrate a birthday, an examination success, a marriage, a new job. All human societies provide rituals for marking birth and death, the two greatest changes of all. Psychoanalysts think that some of their patients suffer from birth trauma, and they can be helped to recall the birth experience and deal with it. Is it possible that there is a similar process when we die – not a dreadful judgement followed by suffering, but wise and compassionate help in making sense of it all? Perhaps the procedure will be more like skilled counselling than a trial. We need to be debriefed, to sort it all out, to see our lives in perspective instead of living through them minute by minute. After death, going back over our actions and our relationships would help us to learn from our earthly lives. We cannot change what has happened, but we can come to understand it. The first stage may be more like being on an analyst's couch than being in the dock, having our sins read out from a long charge sheet.

That may sound like an easy way out, but not to anyone acquainted with the methods of psychoanalysis. It can be a very rigorous and searching process; but God must be at least as compassionate as the average psychoanalyst. The Church has terrified people with visions of hellfire and damnation for far too long. We are told that God is Love. Christians trust that human love survives – love of people, love of animals, love of places.

Science has opened the windows, as Richard Dawkins keeps telling us, but only sufficiently to show us that the universe is marvellously beyond our present comprehension. Many scientists seem to be edging towards a kind of belief, even if they don't like religious language and all the 'baggage' that goes with it. A professor of physics may call himself an agnostic, and refuse to believe in heaven; but suggest to him that it may be possible to replicate the human genome in a parallel universe, and he will think about it.

We have so many unanswered questions. The roots of belief in personal survival, the trust that our questions will be answered, are much older than Richard Dawkins, much older than Charles Darwin. We can find them in the life of simpler societies, where people lived closer to the rhythms of the earth than we do in the age of the mobile telephone and the Internet. We can find them in poetry and literature, which are much more than 'memes'. We can find them in science fiction, though not in the works of Douglas Adams. There is some intelligent guesswork about the next life in the work of another Oxford man, C. S. Lewis.[18]

A new view of evolution

Lewis wrote about the afterlife in allegory – in the last of the children's series that begins with *The Lion, the Witch and the Wardrobe*,[19] and in the second volume of his science fiction trilogy, *Voyage to Venus*. That ends with a scene in which Ransom, the hero, saw

> the relevance of all to all yet more intense, as dimension was added to dimension, and that part of him that could reason and remember was dropped farther and farther behind that part of him which saw, even at the very zenith of complexity, complexity was eaten up and faded . . . and a simplicity beyond all comprehension, ancient and young as spring, drew him with cords of infinite desire into its own stillness.[20]

This passage provides a very interesting reconciliation of Aquinas's conviction that God must be ultimately simple with Richard Dawkins' conviction that God would have to be complex. Lewis once tackled the subject of life after death more directly, in a slim hardback volume entitled *Beyond Personality*.[21] He was writing in the 1940s, towards the end of World War Two, when Richard Dawkins was still a child in East Africa. He accepted the theory of evolution, the long, slow development through millennia of simple life forms into complex ones, and eventually to *Homo sapiens*; but pointed out that there have been major discontinuities in this process that cannot be accounted for by natural selection: animals did not simply become larger, stronger, swifter. They developed brains, and eventually little puny humans developed a moral and spiritual sense. Could that be the next step in evolution: the sloughing off of the body like a chrysalis, and the emergence of pure spirit? The move from *bios* to *zoe*?

CHALLENGING RICHARD DAWKINS

This is a long way from the philosophy of *The Selfish Gene*, though it starts from the same Darwinian premises. It would be interesting to know what Richard Dawkins makes of it. He does, of course, struggle with the discontinuities in biological evolution, but a biologist would find it hard to accept the idea that the next step in evolution outmoded biology.

When this life is over, will we get beyond the space–time continuum, and start finding answers to the ultimate questions? We will have so much to learn. Whatever the wider universe is like, C. S. Lewis must be right about one thing: it will not be static, and it will not be dull. Richard Dawkins will probably be there, asking questions with the rest of us, and pestering the heavenly host for cast-iron proofs. Until then, he must not be allowed to get away with the message that all human life is meaningless and without purpose. He does not have the evidence to prove it.

Key points

- Richard Dawkins' account of his reaction to the death of his friend Douglas Adams shows a genuine sense of loss, but no hope of consolation.
- He argues that because religion has the power to console, it must be false. This is not a sound argument.
- Nobody has the kind of proof he demands about the after-life, but religious belief includes an explanation of why this should be so. Atheism does not.
- The instinctive human reaction is to shy away from death – even at funerals – and to concentrate on living. This seems to be functional.
- The afterlife has traditionally been thought of in terms of punishment and retribution; but there is a move to a more compassionate view, in which we may hope to make sense of our earthly life, and to go on learning.

- C. S. Lewis proposes an evolutionary framework which takes us beyond the physical life (*bios*) through death to spiritual life (*zoe*); but this extension of Darwinsim is unlikely to be acceptable to Richard Dawkins.

Conclusion

Richard Dawkins is not trying to tell the world anything new. There is nothing original in atheism. He is trying to resurrect some very dead controversies about science and religion that scholars resolved well over a century ago. He has no fresh arguments. Atheism does not leave room for argument. It is simply an assertion that God does not exist, end of story.

He says in *The God Delusion* that his views were condemned at a Cambridge conference on science and religion as 'nineteenth century'.[1] He objects that calling something 'nineteenth century' is not the same as saying that it is wrong; and of course he is right about that. Some very good ideas came out of the nineteenth century, and the evolution debate was one of them; but he does not even understand what that debate was about in its original nineteenth-century context. He tells his readers that Charles Darwin 'seized the window of the burka and wrenched it open, letting in a flood of understanding whose dazzling novelty and power to uplift the human spirit perhaps had no precedent'.[2]

To put it mildly, that is overstating the case. Darwin did not invent the concept of evolution, nor did he develop gene theory. In *The Selfish Gene*, Richard Dawkins notes, 'Darwin, if he read this book, would scarcely recognise his own original theory in it.'[3]

There are still gaps in evolutionary theory, though it is the best theory we have on the origins of the human race. We have not found the 'missing link'. Chimpanzees and humans cannot interbreed. Richard Dawkins thinks that gap is 'regrettable', but he has no real hopes of bridging it. Similarly, he would like to bridge the gap between inanimate matter and living things, but he cannot do more than to imagine that crystals have feelings.

He writes with an engaging passion, but he often uses words to conceal rather than to reveal. 'Just as . . .' is used repeatedly to suggest that two subjects are like each other when they are manifestly different. Genes are not 'Chicago gangsters'. Islam is not 'analogous to a carnivorous gene complex', and Buddhism to 'a herbivorous one'.[4] These are not even generalizations: they involve bending the meanings of words. His entry on the Oxford University website calls him 'the first true ethologist of the gene'. Can that be his own description of his academic work? The dictionary will not support him. Ethology is the science of character formation in human beings. The term is derived from the Greek word *ethos*. By extension, it is used to refer to the study of animal behaviour; but what can he mean by the ethology of the *gene*? This is doing violence to language.

He insists that he is speaking for science, but scientists do not fling words about in this careless and imprecise way; and it is evident that he does not speak for the scientific community as a whole. He claims that eminent scientists share his religious views. A reference to their own comments on the subject suggest that they do not.

From the evidence of his writings, he seems professionally very isolated. Most scholars of his seniority have colleagues with whom they share ideas. They work in groups. They quote each other's papers, publish jointly with their brighter students, acknowledge each other's contributions to thinking out particular problems. Richard Dawkins does not appear to work with other scientists. Nor does he seem to interact with other members of the academic community, except to disagree with the theologians. He knows that human vision is limited; but he persistently distorts and misrepresents religion, sometimes at a childish level.

He is an Oxford professor. Oxford is a very hospitable place to its own. Social life in the colleges is arranged so that academics continually meet people with different kinds of expertise and different views – in senior common rooms, at formal dinners and garden parties, at gatherings for distinguished visitors. It would seem almost impossible for an Oxford don to dismiss all subjects other than science as 'memes' – to fail to learn something from classicists, historians, geographers, philosophers, anthropologists, psychologists, economists, politicists, sociologists, palaeontologists and all the others whose knowledge and skills are on his doorstep or available on his computer. He can raid every library in the world on the Internet, yet there are vast gaps in his reading.

He restricts 'evolution' to its biological meaning, refusing to admit that there are other kinds of evolution – the evolution of religious ideas, the evolution of moral standards. He restricts research methodology to the pure sciences, ignoring the fact that the formulation and testing of successive hypotheses is basic to any kind of academic study.

He has no feeling for human groups, and the way they evolve painfully over centuries. He does not understand tradition – or the difference between myth and history, or the difference between history and science fiction. Having invested Charles Darwin with absolute authority (Darwin would be amazed, and probably rather troubled), he attacks what he considers to be the views of religious extremists while ignoring all rational debate and balanced judgement. In a word, he caters to ignorance and prejudice.

He opposes religious intolerance, and at a time when the Western world is facing unprecedented terrorist attacks, that makes good reading for frightened people; but he is highly intolerant of any views other than his own. When Sir Karl Popper was a very old man, he gave a lecture on Toleration. A member of the audience asked him, 'What should the tolerant not tolerate?' and his answer, clear and immediate in response, was 'Intolerance'. By that standard, Richard Dawkins falls short of civilized standards in a democratic society. He insists that he is not a confrontational person. Perhaps he simply enjoys taking an extreme position for the sake of argument.

Is his writing dangerous? Probably not. We value freedom of speech, and those of us who disagree with him are free to answer him as we think fit. I am a Christian, but I have tried to get beyond the boundaries of my own faith to see what religion means for the whole human race. I have argued that the existence of the universe presupposes the existence of an intelligent Creator; that this alone gives meaning and purpose to human life; that human beings are capable of being touched by the power of their Creator; that the basic problem of free will, how we abuse it and how we can be redeemed by God in action, is one for all humankind, for people of all faiths; that what Christians call the Holy Spirit – the spirit of peace and social justice – is available not only to Christians, but is the only hope for a divided and desperate world; that the next step in evolution is not bigger and better computers, but the evolution of the human spirit beyond the confines of the space–time continuum.

Many millions of Christians, Jews, Muslims, Hindus, Buddhists and members of other faiths will go on debating these issues among themselves, agreeing on some things and disagreeing about others. They will do so in many languages and many cultures, in literature and poetry and song. They do not, like atheists, all have to subscribe to the same bleak and hopeless denial.

Richard Dawkins blames religion for our terrors and our

problems; but they do not come from religion. They come from the animal part of our nature – the snarling retreat from attack, and the instinct to make a pre-emptive strike. They come from fear – fear of instability, fear of change, and in a nuclear age, fear of annihilation; but we are more than animals, and we can go on asking questions. If that first ape descendant really did make history by climbing down out of the trees and standing erect, I am willing to bet that the first thing she did was to look up at the sun, and to ask how it got there.

Abbreviations

Richard Dawkins' books are referred to as follows:

SG   *The Selfish Gene*
RE   *River out of Eden*
BW *The Blind Watchmaker*
UR *Unweaving the Rainbow*
DC *A Devil's Chaplain*
GD *The God Delusion*

References to the Bible are to the New Standard Revised Version, 1998, (NSRV) unless otherwise noted. AV is the Authorised or King James Version of 1611.

'Commemoration (A)' refers to the entry for an individual in the Anglican Calendar in *Common Worship* (Church House Publishing, 2000). These are indexed by date in *The Saints of the Anglican Calendar* (Canterbury Press, 2000), with source notes.

'Commemoration (RC)' refers to the entry for an individual in the Roman Catholic Calendar. The most up-to-date comprehensive source in English is *Butler's Lives of the Saints*, ed. Paul Burns, 12 vols (January–December) (Burns and Oates/Continuum, 1997–99), which similarly provides source notes.

Notes

1 The World of Richard Dawkins

1 *The Selfish Gene* (30th anniversary edition, 2006), p. 35.

2 *Unweaving the Rainbow* (1998), p. 12

3 *The God Delusion* (2006), p. 361.

4 See (on the Oxford University website) http://www.simonyi. oc.acc.uk.dawkins/World of Dawkins-archive/Biography and http:// en.wikipedia.org/wiki.Richard Dawkins

5 *GD*, p. 11.

6 *A Devil's Chaplain* (2003), pp. 225–6.

7 *DC*, p. 8.

8 *GD*, p. 11.

9 *DC*, p. 8.

10 See Kathleen Jones, *The Making of Social Policy in Britain* (3rd edn, 2000), ch. 11: 'Breaking the Consensus'.

11 *DC*, pp. 104–6.

12 Konrad Lorenz (1903–89) founded the ethological school of animal behaviour under natural conditions, in the University of Vienna. He is 'widely regarded as the father of ethology', according to *Chambers' Biological Dictionary*.

13 *UR*, pp. xiv–xv.

14 See http://www.edge/org/3rd_culture/bios/simonyi/html and http://en.wikipedia.org/wiki/Charles Simonyi

15 *GD*, p. 3.

16 ibid.

17 *GD*, p. 5.

18 *The Blind Watchmaker* (1986), p. 44.

19 *BW*, pp. 290–1.

20 Francis Darwin, *The Life of Charles Darwin* (1902), p. 239.

21 Gregor Johann Mendel (1822–84) was born the son of a peasant farmer in Silesia; he was ordained priest at the age of 25 and

became a monk of the Augustinian cloister of Brunn, Austria, where he became abbot in 1868.

22 *GD*, p. 99.

23 *DC*, p. 79.

24 *DC*, pp.20–6 and 78–90.

25 *DC*, pp. 24.

26 *River Out of Eden* (1995), pp. 45–57.

27 As Richard Dawkins points out, *homo* in Latin means a human being, and the corresponding terms for a man and a woman are *vir* and *femina*.

28 *SG*, p. 193.

29 ibid.

30 *SG*, p. 1.

31 *DC*, pp. 117–27.

32 *DC*, p. 137.

33 William Paley, *Natural Theology: On Evidence of the Existence and Attributes of the Deity* (1802).

34 *BW*, p. 44.

35 *BW*, pp. 4–5.

36 *UR*, p. 193.

37 Douglas Adams, *The Hitch-Hiker's Guide to the Galaxy*, *The Restaurant at the End of the Universe* and *So Long, and Thanks for All the Fish*. First written as a radio series in 1978, *HHGG* was transferred to television, extended and then published in paperbacks.

38 *DC*, p. 170.

39 *GD*, pp. 362–3.

40 *GD*, p. 363.

2 Out of the Cosmic Soup

1 Bill Bryson, *A Short History of Nearly Everything* (2003), p. 31.

2 *The God Delusion* (2006), p. 149–50.

3 See a discussion on coincidences and probability in *The Blind Watchmaker* (1986), pp. 159–62.

4 *GD*, pp. 12–19.

5 Albert Einstein, *Out of My Later Years* (Wings Books 1996), pp. 19–25.

6 Quoted on the title page of Paul Davies' *God and the New Physics* (1983).

7 *GD*, p. 14.

8 Martin Rees, *Before the Beginning* (1997), p. 6.

9 For this story, see a very lively chapter in Bryson, *A Short History*, pp. 480–501.

10 *GD*, p. 99.

11 ibid.

12 *GD*, pp. 101–2.

13 See Martin Rees, *Before the Beginning*, pp. 31–52.

14 Psalm 93 (AV).

15 John Habgood, later Archbishop of York, had a doctorate in physiology. His *Religion and Science* (1964) is a careful and open-minded study. The Vatican Observatory report *Physics, Philosophy and Theology* (1988) includes a long and rigorous analysis by Fr R. J. Clifford SJ of creation doctrines, quantum theory and much else of relevance to the Dawkins thesis.

16 *A Devil's Chaplain* (2003), p. 18.

17 *Unweaving the Rainbow* (1998), p. 179.

18 *The Blind Watchmaker* (1986), p. xi.

19 *DC*, p. 149.

20 *BW*, p. 151.

21 One of the chief exponents of string theory is the Japanese cosmologist Michio Kaku. See *A Scientific Odyssey through Parallel Universes, Time Warps and the Tenth Dimension* (1999).

22 *GD*, pp. 152–3. See also pp. 19, 99, 285.

23 Paul Davies, *The Goldilocks Enigma* (2006), pp. 295–303. This subject is also discussed by Fr Clifford in the Vatican Observatory report.

24 *GD*, p. 158.

25 *GD*, pp. 103–5. Blaise Pascal (1623–62), author of the *Pensées*.

26 *GD*, p. 155.

27 *DC*, pp. 149.

3 Asking Reasonable Questions

1 *A Devil's Chaplain* (2003), pp. 241–8 – 'A Prayer for My Daughter: Good and Bad Reasons for Believing'.

2 Carl Gustav Jung (1875–1961), *The Psychology of the Unconscious* (1911–12) and other works.

3 There is some historical basis in the account by Gildas of a *dux Britannicorum* who rallied the resistance to Viking invasion about the year 500 – but not in circumstances of fifteenth-century chivalry.

4 *The Blind Watchmaker* (1986), p. 21.

NOTES

5 *The Selfish Gene* (2006), p. 198.

6 1225–74. For the life of Aquinas, see F. C. Copleston, *Aquinas* (1955), and G. K. Chesterton, *Saint Thomas Aquinas* (2000), a short but illuminating essay. Complete works in Latin, Parma edn, 25 vols (1852–72; reprinted New York, 1948). English translations include *The Summa Theologica*, 22 vols (1912–26), and *The Summa Contra Gentiles*, 5 vols (1928-29). T. Gilby (trans. and ed.), *St Thomas Aquinas: Philosophical Texts* (Oxford University Press 1951). Commemoration (A and RC) 28 January.

7 Each argument is numbered, which makes reference easy when his system is understood: thus '*ST* 2a, 2e, 34, 2, ad 1' means the *Summa Theologica, Secunda Secundae* (i.e. the second part of the second book), question 34, second reply to the first objection.

8 *GD*, p. 79.

9 *ST* 1a, xxxii, 1 and 2.

10 *ST* 1a, 2 ii, ad 1.

11 *Unweaving the Rainbow* (1998), p. x.

12 *ST* 1a, xii, 1.

13 *The God Delusion* (2006), p.312.

14 *GD*, p. 314.

15 Nicholas Ridley and Hugh Latimer were burned at the stake in 1555; commemoration (A) 1 December. Archbishop Cranmer followed them a year later; commemoration (A) 21 March.

16 Richard Whiting, Hugh Faringdon and John Beche; commemoration (RC) 1 December.

17 Thomas More and John Fisher; commemoration (RC and A) 6 July.

18 Edmund Campion and Alexander Briant; commemoration (RC) 1 December.

19 Francis Bacon, Baron Verulam of Verulam, was Lord Chancellor from 1618 to 1626.

20 Immanuel Kant (1724–1804) was Professor of Logic and Metaphysics in the University of Königsberg, then in Prussia and now in Poland.

21 *GD*, p. 224.

22 *GD*, p. 232.

23 Sir Karl Popper (1902–94) was Professor of Logic at the London School of Economics and author of *The Logic of Scientific Discovery* (1959), *Objective Knowledge* (1972), *The Open Society and Its Enemies* (1945), *Unended Quest* (1976) and *The Poverty of Historicism* (1957).

24 *DC,* p. 196.
25 Bryan Magee, *Popper* (1973).
26 Popper, *Objective Knowledge,* p. 145.
27 Popper, *Objective Knowledge,* p. 145.
28 *UR,* p. 21.
29 *UR,* p. 31.

4 God of Our Fathers

1 Qur'an, surah 3, 7.
2 *The God Delusion* (2006), p. 31. 'Filicidal' means killing one's own son, a reference to the death of Jesus Christ.
3 *GD,* p. 251.
4 *GD,* pp. 237–8.
5 *GD,* p. 242. Genesis 22.1–17.
6 *GD,* p. 238.
7 ibid.
8 *GD,* pp. 237–8.
9 Many accounts of creation from other cultures are summarized in Ellen van Wolde, *Stories of the Beginnning: Genesis 1—11 and other Creation Stories* (1996).
10 Genesis 16.
11 Genesis 27.
12 2 Samuel 11.2–15.
13 *GD,* p. 36.
14 William Tyndale (*c.* 1494–1536): commemoration 6 October (Anglican Church).
15 Spain was the most powerful Catholic country in Europe, but by 1569, the *Santa Biblia* had been translated into Spanish by Casiodoro de Reina, and approved by Church and king; St Teresa of Avila and St John of the Cross certainly read the Bible in their own language as well as in Latin.
16 Radio 4 (21 January 2007) and newspaper accounts.
17 *The Blind Watchmaker* (1986), p. 284.
18 *BW,* p. 293.
19 BBC 2, *Horizon,* 26 January 2006.
20 *GD,* p. 132. The full discussion is on pp. 129–33.
21 *GD,* p. 82n.
22 *GD,* pp. 331–7.
23 *Sunday Times,* 31 December 2006.

24 *GD*, pp. 331–7.

25 *GD*, pp. 341–3. This list seems to owe something to Melvyn Bragg's *The Adventure of English* (2003), chs 9 and 10.

26 Jimmy Carter, *Our Endangered Values* (2005) p. 48.

27 *Deus Caritas Est: Encyclical Letter of the Supreme Pontiff Benedict XVI to the Bishops, Priests and Deacons, Men and Women Religious and all the Lay Faithful on Christian Love* (2005).

28 See Genesis 1.26–28 and Genesis 2.20–23 respectively.

29 *Tablet*, 2 June 2007.

5 Down to Earth

1 *The God Delusion* (2006), p. 250.

2 *GD*, p. 94.

3 See William Temple, *Readings in St John's Gospel* (1939) for a discussion on authorship.

4 *GD*, p. 93.

5 *GD*, pp. 178–9.

6 Isaiah 9.6–7.

7 *GD*, p. 206.

8 Matthew 7.16–20.

9 Eusebius, *Historia Ecclesiastica*, chs 4, 8 and 16–18. A. L. Williams (trans. and ed.), *Justin Martyr: The Dialogue with Trypho* (1930).

10 The Doctrine of the Immaculate Conception was defined by Pope Pius IX in 1854.

11 Matthew 16.15–17.

12 Matthew 6.7–15.

13 Mark 16.19.

14 *GD*, p. 178.

15 Luke 2.41–50.

16 John 2.1–11.

17 *GD*, p. 250.

18 Matthew 15.22–28.

19 *GD*, p. 253.

20 Kenotic theory: see *The Oxford Concise Dictionary of the Christian Church* (1977, 1996 edn), pp. 286–7.

21 Matthew 10.9–10; Mark 6.8–9; Luke 9.3.

22 John 8.3–11.

23 Matthew 4.1–11; Mark 1.12–13; Luke 4.1–13.

24 Matthew 22.37–39; Mark 12.30–31; Luke 10.27.

25 Luke 10.25–37.

26 Matthew 14.25–33; Mark 4.35–41.

27 Matthew 21.12–13; Mark 11.15–17.

28 Matthew 23.*passim*.

29 Matthew 26.61; 27.40; Mark 14.57–58; John 2.18–21.

30 Matthew 21.6–11; Mark 11.8–10.

31 Matthew 26.26–29; Mark 14.22–25; Luke 22.17–20.

32 Matthew 26.36–46; Mark 14.32–42; Luke 22.39–46.

33 Matthew 26.14–16, 47–50; Mark 14.10–11, 43–46; Luke 6.16; 22.3–5, 47–55; John 13.21–29; 18.3–5; Acts 1.16–21.

34 *GD*, pp. 252–3. See Tom Wright, *Judas and the Gospel of Jesus* (2005).

35 *GD*, p. 251.

36 Matthew 27.11–56; Mark 15.25–39; Luke 23.33–49; John 19.17–30.

37 Socrates the Historian, *Historia Ecclesiastica*, 1:17; Sozomen, *Historia Ecclesiastica*, Book 2.1. For what is known about Helena, see Kathleen Jones, *Women Saints: Lives of Faith and Courage* (1999); her commemoration is on 21 May in the Roman Catholic and Anglican Churches.

38 Hymn 332 in *Hymns Ancient and Modern*.

39 See p. 35.

40 Matthew 28.1–9; Mark 16.1–8; Luke 24.1–12; John 20.1–18.

41 John 20.24–29.

42 John 21.9–13.

43 1 Corinthians 15.6.

44 Mark 16.12–13; Luke 24.13–32.

45 Matthew 28.16–20; Mark 16.14–16; Luke 24.49.

46 Mark 16.19; Luke 24.51; Acts 1.6–11.

47 Luke 24.52.

48 John 21.24.

49 Their feast days are Matthew, 21 September; Mark, 25 April; Luke, 18 October; John, 27 December (all in both A and RC).

50 1 John 1–13.

6 Being Nice to People

1 *The God Delusion* (2006), pp. 216–21.

2 Acts 2.1–11.

3 Acts 2.14–36.

4 John 3.8.

5 John 16.13.

6 1 Corinthians 2.10.

7 Galatians 5.16.

8 *GD*, pp. 34–5.

9 The apostle Thomas: commemoration 3 July.

10 Genesis 8.8–12.

11 Matthew 28.19.

12 John 10.16.

13 Acts 8.27–39.

14 Acts 10.9–16.

15 Galatians 2.*passim*.

16 Acts 8.18–23.

17 *GD*, p. 37.

18 *GD*, p. 257.

19 Acts 7.58; 9.1–30; commemoration 29 June (A and RC).

20 Isaiah 11.2.

21 Galatians 5.22.

22 See Frances Young, *The Making of the Creeds* (1991).

23 Pope Damasus I: commemoration 11 December (RC). Jerome: commemoration 30 September (A and RC).

24 Irenaeus of Lyons (*c*. 130–200): commemoration 28 June (A and RC).

25 *GD*, p. 97.

26 Acts 2.14–36.

27 Acts 7.*passim*.

28 Michael Baigent, Richard Leigh and Henry Lincoln, *Holy Blood, Holy Grail* (1982).

29 As part of the Nag Hammadi Papers. See Esther de Boer, *Mary Magdalene: Beyond the Myth* (1996), which gives a full provenance.

30 *The Gospel of Thomas*, trans. and ed. Stevan Davies (2003).

31 *The Lost Books of the Bible*, with an Introduction by Solomon J. Schepps (1979), contains a number of the shorter accounts, but the title is somewhat misleading, since the collection does not include the longer and better-known ones.

32 *The Lost Gospels*, BBC 4, 4 December 2005.

33 *GD*, pp. 92–4.

34 The entry is through St Catherine's Church in Manger Square, next to the Church of the Nativity.

35 Matthew 16.18.

36 *GD*, pp. 226–30.

7 Imagine . . .

1 *The God Delusion* (2006), p. 222.

2 *GD*, p. 166.

3 *GD*, pp. 1–2.

4 There was a terrible example of this process in York in 1192, when the entire Jewish community was besieged in the castle, men, women and children, and committed suicide. In 1992, Christians and Jews held a memorial on the site in reparation.

5 The author was a member of Lord Gardiner's Committee on Human Rights and Terrorism in Northern Ireland, and was involved in many discussions with both Republican and Unionist prisoners. See official report, HMSO, Cmnd. 5847 (1975).

6 *A Devil's Chaplain* (2003), p. 158.

7 *DC*, p. 154.

8 Rowan Williams, *Writing in the Dust: Reflections on 11th September and its Aftermath* (2002).

9 *DC*, p. 160.

10 *GD*, p. 260.

11 See Kai Erikson, 'Notes on the Sociology of Deviance', pp. 9–21, and J. R. Kitsuse, 'Societal Reaction to Deviant Behavior: Problems of Theory and Method', both in Howard S. Becker, *The Other Side: Perspectives on Deviance* (1964).

12 *GD*, pp. 248–9.

13 *GD*, p. 215.

14 *GD*, p. 221.

15 *GD*, pp. 265–72.

16 *GD*, p. 269.

17 *GD*, pp. 31, 34, 38, 42–3, 94 and elsewhere.

18 See John Rawls, *A Theory of Justice* (1980, rev. edn 1999); Bruce Ackerman, *Social Justice in the Liberal State* (1980); Ian Brownlie, *Basic Documents in Human Rights* (5th edn 2006).

19 *Church Times*, 10 June 2005.

20 Rowan Williams, *Christ on Trial* (2002). Quoted by Mike Higson in *Difficult Gospel: the Theology of Rowan Williams* (2004), p. 117.

21 Rowan Williams, *Open to Judgement* (1995, 2002), quoted in

Higson, *Difficult Gospel*, pp. 117–18.

  22 Matthew 25.34–45.

  23 *GD*, p. 166.

8 What's Wrong with the World?

  1 *The God Delusion* (2006), p. 306.

  2 Steve Jones, *In the Blood: God, Genes and Destiny* (1996). See especially ch. VI.

  3 *GD*, p. 252.

  4 Romans 7.19.

  5 Exodus 20.2–17.

  6 Matthew 22.34–40. See also Matthew 19.19 and Luke 10.23.

  7 Luke 23.34.

  8 The Dalai Lama, *The Universe as a Single Atom: How Science and Spirituality Can Serve Our World* (2005). An earlier book, *The Path to Freedom: Freedom in Exile and Ancient Wisdom in the Modern World* (2002), won the Nobel Prize. The Dalai Lama writes in English.

  9 See John Allen, *Rabble-Rouser for Peace: The Autobiography of Desmind Tutu* (2006), pp. 342–71.

  10 See Paul van Tongeren *et al.* (eds.), *People Building Peace II: Successful Stories of Civil Society* (2005); Ted Robert Gurr, *Peace and Conflict: A Detailed Study of Armed Conflicts, Self-Determination Movements and Democracy* (2002).

  11 Jones, *In the Blood*, p. 269.

  12 *A Devil's Chaplain* (2003), p. 8.

  13 Romans 8.22 (NSRV).

  14 *The Blind Watchmaker* (1986), p. 159.

  15 John 1.10.

  16 *Out of the Silent Planet* (1938), *Perelandra* (1943) and *That Hideous Strength* (1945).

  17 Revelation 12.7–12.

  18 *GD*, p. 257.

  19 *The Book of Revelation*, trans. J. B. Phillips (1957).

9 Next

  1 *The God Delusion* (2006), pp. 347–52.

  2 *GD* pp. 354–5.

3 *A Devil's Chaplain* (2003), p. 167.

4 *DC*, pp. 163.

5 *DC*, pp. 165–7.

6 From W. H. Auden's poem, recited with great effect in the film *Four Weddings and a Funeral*.

7 *GD* p. 117.

8 *DC*, pp. 179–86,

9 *GD*, p. 352.

10 I have not come across any Chinese speculation about Righteous Woman.

11 *GD*, p. 357.

12 *DC*, p. 163.

13 John 14.2.

14 *GD*, p. 130n.

15 *GD*, p. 358.

16 John Henry Newman (1801–90); commemoration (A and RC) 11 August.

17 1 Corinthians 15.51–52.

18 C. S. Lewis (1898–1963). See Humphrey Carpenter, *The Inklings: C. S. Lewis, J. R. R. Tolkien, Charles Williams and their Friends* (1979); Roger Lancelyn Green and Walter Hooper, *C. S. Lewis: A Biography* (1974); George Sayer, *Jack: A Life of C. S. Lewis* (1988). Most of C. S. Lewis's theological works have been republished in successive paperback editions by Fontana.

19 C. S. Lewis, *The Last Battle* (Bodley Head 1956).

20 Ch. 17 of *Perelandra* (1943). Now published by Pan Books as *Voyage to Venus* (1953) and other editions.

21 C. S. Lewis, *Beyond Personality: The Christian Idea of God* (1944). This has not been republished as a separate book, but is now included (in a shortened and somewhat emasculated form) as the last chapter of *Mere Christianity* (originally published in 1952). The 1944 edition should be consulted for the full argument about evolution.

Conclusion

1 *The God Delusion* (2006), p. 156.

2 *GD*, p. 367.

3 *The Selfish Gene* (2006), p. 195.

4 *GD*, p. 200.

Select Bibliography

Since Richard Dawkins' writing touches on many different areas of academic study, there is a very large literature which is relevant. The following list consists only of books quoted, referred to, or specifically consulted in writing the present study. Many of them have their own lengthy bibliographies.

Ackerman, Bruce, *Social Justice in the Liberal State*, Yale University Press, 1980.

Adamnan, *Adamnan's Life of Columba*, ed. Richard Sharpe, Penguin, 1991.

Adams, Douglas, *The Hitch-Hiker's Guide to the Galaxy, The Restaurant at the End of the Universe*, and *So Long, and Thanks for All the Fish*. First written as a radio series in 1978, transferred to television, and then published in paperback editions by Pan Books.

Allen, John, *Rabble-Rouser for Peace: The Authorized Biography of Desmond Tutu*, Free Press, Simon and Schuster, 2006.

Bacon, Francis, *The New Atlantis* (1624), in *The Philosophical Works of Francis Bacon*, ed. J. M. Robertson, Routledge, 1905, pp. 712–32.

Baigent, Michael, Leigh, Richard and Lincoln, Henry, *Holy Blood, Holy Grail*, Random House, 1982.

Baigent, Michael, *The Jesus Papers*, HarperCollins, 2006.

Becker, Howard S., *The Other Side: Perspectives on Deviance*, Free Press, Glencoe, 1964.

Bloom, Jonathan and Blair, Sheila, *Islam: A Thousand Years of Faith and Power*, Yale University Press, 2002.

Boer, Esther de, *Mary Magdalene: Beyond the Myth*, trans. John Bowden, SCM Press, 1996.

Boulay, Shirley du, *Beyond the Darkness: A Biography of Bede Griffiths*, Rider/Random House, 1998.

Bragg, Melvyn, *The Adventure of English*, Hodder and Stoughton, 2003.

Brownlie, Ian, *Basic Documents on Human Rights*, Oxford University Press, 5th edn, 2006.

Bryson, Bill, *A Short History of Nearly Everything,* Doubleday, 2003; Black Swan edn, 2004.

Butler's Lives of the Saints, 12 vols: new edn, 12 vols, ed. Paul Burns, Burns and Oates, 1995–99.

Carpenter, Humphrey, *The Inklings: C. S. Lewis, J. R. R. Tolkien, Charles Williams and their Friends*, Allen and Unwin, 1979.

Carter, Jimmy, *Our Endangered Values: America's Moral Crisis*, Simon and Schuster, 2005.

Chadwick, Henry, *The Early Church*, Penguin, 1967.

Chesterton, G. K., *St Thomas Aquinas*, new edn in *Chesterton Biographies*, House of Stratus, 2000.

Cleary, Thomas (ed.), *The Teachings of Zen*, Shambala, Massachusetts, USA, 1998.

Dalai Lama, *The Universe in a Single Atom*, Little Brown, 2005.

Darwin, Charles, *The Origin of Species by Means of Natural Selection* (1859), Oxford University Press, 1998 edn.

Darwin, Charles, *The Descent of Man and Selection in Relation to Sex*, Murray, 2nd edn, 1905.

Darwin, Francis, *The Life of Charles Darwin* (includes Charles Darwin's own brief account of his early life and his discoveries), 1902, repub. Senate/Tiger Books, 1995.

Davies, Stevan (trans. and ed.), *The Gospel of Thomas*, Darton, Longman and Todd, 2003.

Davies, Paul, *God and the New Physics*, Penguin, 1983.

Davies, Paul, *The Mind of God*, Penguin, 1993.

Davies, Paul, *The Goldilocks Enigma*, Allen Lane, 2006.

Dawkins, Richard, *The Selfish Gene,* Oxford University Press, 1976; 30th anniversary edition, 2006.

Dawkins, Richard, *The Blind Watchmaker*, Penguin, 1986.

Dawkins, Richard, *River Out of Eden: A Darwinian View of Life*, Weidenfeld and Nicolson, 1995.

Dawkins, Richard, *Climbing Mount Improbable*, Norton, 1996.

Dawkins, Richard, *Unweaving the Rainbow: Science, Delusion and the Appetite for Wonder*, Penguin, 1998.

Dawkins, Richard, *A Devil's Chaplain*, Weidenfeld and Nicolson, 2003.

Dawkins, Richard, *The God Delusion*, Bantam Press, 2006.

Dehaene, Stanislaus, *The Number Sense: How the Mind Creates Mathematics,* Penguin Books, 1999.

Ehrman, Bart D., *Lost Scriptures: Books that Did Not Make It into the New Testament*, Oxford University Press, 2003.

Einstein, Albert, *Out of My Later Years: The Scientist, Philosopher and Man Portrayed through His Own Words*, Random House/ Wings, New York, 1950.

Erikson, Kai T., 'Notes on the Sociology of Deviance', in Howard S. Becker, *The Other Side* (see Becker).

Eusebius, *Historia Ecclesiastica*, Penguin edn, *The History of the Church from Christ to Constantine*, trans. G. A. Williamson, 1965, rev. edn, 1989.

Freud, Sigmund, *Group Psychology and the Analysis of the Ego*, Norton, New York, 1959.

Gibbon, Edward, *The Decline and Fall of the Roman Empire*, Intro. Hugh Trevor-Roper, David Campbell, 1993.

Gilgamesh, *The Epic of Gilgamesh*, trans. N. K. Sandars, Penguin Epics, 2006.

Goffman, Erving, *Asylums: Essays on the Social Situation of Mental Patients and Other Inmates*, Anchor Books, Doubleday, 1961.

Goffman, Erving, *Stigma: Notes on the Management of Spoiled Identity* (1963), Penguin, 1968.

Gollancz, Victor and Greene, Barbara, *God of a Hundred Names: Prayers of Many Peoples and Creeds*, Hodder and Stoughton, 1962.

Graham, A. C. (ed.), *Poems of the Late T'ang*, Penguin Classics, 1965.

Green, Roger Lancelyn and Hooper, Walter, *C. S. Lewis: A Biography*, Collins, 1974.

Greene, Brian, *The Fabric of the Cosmos*, Allen Lane, 2004.

Greene, Mark, *Cracking the Code*, London Institute for Contemporary Christianity, 2004.

Gumbel, Nicky, *The Da Vinci Code: A Response*, Alpha International, 2005.

Gurr, Ted Robert, *Peace and Conflict: A Detailed Study of Armed Conflict, Self-determination Movements and Democracy*, University of Maryland Center for International Development and Conflict Management, 2001.

Habgood, John, *Religion and Science*, Hodder and Stoughton, 1964.

Hawking, Stephen, *A Brief History of Time: From the Big Bang to the Black Hole*, Bantam Books, 1988.

Hawking, Stephen, *The Universe in a Nutshell*, Bantam Press, 2001.

Higton, Mike, *Difficult Gospel: The Theology of Rowan Williams*, SCM Press, 2004.

Hodge, Stephen (ed.), *Tao Te Ching*, Godsfield Press, Alresford, 2002.

Ipgrave, Michael (ed.), *The Road Ahead: A Christian–Muslim Dialogue,* Church House Publishing, 2002.

Irenaeus of Lyons, *Adversus haereses: Against Heresies*, trans. and ed. F. R. M. Hitchcock, 1898.

John of Damascus, *De Fide Orthodoxa*, Eng. trans. by S. D. F. Salmond, in P. Schaff and H. Wace, *The Nicene and Post-Nicene Christian Fathers* (1887–1900), vol. 9 (1899), repub. Grand Rapids, Michigan, 1979.

Jones, Kathleen, *The Compassionate Society*, SPCK, 1966.

Jones, Kathleen, 'Perspectives on Deviancy' in Kathleen Jones, John Brown and Jonathan Bradshaw, *Issues in Social Policy*, Routledge and Kegan Paul, 1978.

Jones, Kathleen, *The Making of Social Policy in Britain: From the Poor Law to New Labour*, 1994, rev. edn, Athlone Press, 2000.

Jones, Kathleen, *Women Saints: Lives of Faith and Courage*, Burns and Oates, 1999.

Jones, Kathleen, *Saints of the Anglican Calendar*, Canterbury Press, 2000.

Jones, Steve, *In the Blood: God, Genes and Destiny*, HarperCollins, 1996.

Jung, Carl Gustav, *Man and his Symbols*, trans. and ed. D. A. Hill, Doubleday, 1964.

Kaku, Michio, *A Scientific Odyssey through Parallel Universes, Time Warps and the Tenth Dimension*, Oxford University Press, 1999.

Kant, Immanuel, *The Critique of Pure Reason*, 1781, trans. and ed. P. Guyen and E. Matthews, Cambridge University Press, New York, 1976.

Kant, Immanuel, *The Critique of Practical Reason* (1788), trans. E. W. Beck, Garland, New York, 1976.

Kant, Immanuel, *The Critique of Judgement* (1790), trans. and ed. P. Guyen and E. Matthews, Cambridge University Press, New York, 2001.

Kelly, J. N. D., *Early Christian Doctrines*, Adam and Charles Black, 1980.

Kelly, J. N. D., *The Oxford Dictionary of Popes*, Oxford University Press, 1996.

Kent, Adam, *British Social Movements since 1945: Sex, Colour, Peace and Power*, Palgrave, Basingstoke, 2001.

Kitcher, Philip, *Abusing Science: The Case against Creationism*, MIT Press, Cambridge, Mass., 1982.

Koran, see Qur'an.

Küng, Hans, *Credo*, trans. John Bowden, SCM Press, 1992.

Lewis, C. S., *Out of the Silent Planet*, John Lane, 1938.

Lewis, C. S. *Perelandra*, John Lane, 1943. Reprinted by Pan Books as *Voyage to Venus*, 1953.

Lewis, C. S., *Beyond Personality: The Christian Idea of God*, Geoffrey Bles, 1944.

Lewis, C. S., *That Hideous Strength*, John Lane, 1945.

Lewis, C. S., *Mere Christianity*, Geoffrey Bles, 1952.

Lewis, C. S., *The Great Divorce: A Dream*, Geoffrey Bles, 1953. (All the above books by C. S. Lewis are in modern paperback editions.)

McGrath, Alister, *Dawkins' God: Genes, Memes and the Meaning of Life*, Blackball, 2004.

McGrath, Alister and McGrath, J. C., *The Dawkins Delusion: Atheist Fundamentalism and the Denial of the Divine*, SPCK, 2007.

Magee, Bryan, *Popper*, HarperCollins Fontana, 1973.

Malleus Maleficarum, The Hammer of the Witches, Heinrich Institutoris and Jacobus Sprenger, trans. and ed. Christopher S. Mackay, Cambridge University Press, 2006.

Mandeville, John, *The Travels of Sir John Mandeville*, Penguin, 2005.

Meisel, Sandra, *The Da Vinci Hoax: Exposing the Errors in the Da Vinci Code*, Ignatius Press, 2004.

Merton, Thomas, *The Way of Chuang Tzu*, Burns and Oates, 1965.

More, Thomas, *Utopia*, trans. and intro. Paul Turner, Penguin Books, 1965. Murray, Margaret, *God of the Witches*, Oxford University Press, 1970.

Nazir Ali, Michael, with Stone, Christopher, *Understanding My Islamic Neighbour*, Canterbury Press, 2002.

Nicholson, Reynold A., *Mystics of Islam*, Arkana, Penguin Books, 1989 (first published by George Bell and Sons Ltd., 1914).

Ohlsen, Carl and Oldenbourg, Zoe, *Massacre at Monségur: A History of the Albigensian Crusades*, Phoenix Press, 2001.

Oxford Concise Dictionary of the Christian Churches, ed. E. A. Livingstone, Oxford University Press, 1977.

Paley, William, *Natural Theology: On Evidence of the Existence and Attributes of the Deity*, 1802.

Patrologia Latina, 221 vols, ed. J. P. Migne, Paris, 1844–64.

Penrose, Roger, *The Road to Reality: A Complete Guide to the Physical Universe*, Jonathan Cape/Random House, 2004.

Phillips, J. B., *Letters to Young Churches*, Fontana, 1955.

Phillips, J. B. (trans.), *The Book of Revelation*, Geoffrey Bles, 1997.

Polkinghorne, John, *Reason and Reality in Relationship to Science and Theology*, SPCK, 1991.

Pollak, Robert, *Signs of Life: The Language and Meaning of DNA*, Penguin, 1985.

Popper, Karl, *The Open Society and Its Enemies*, Routledge and Kegan Paul, 2 vols, 1945, 5th edn, 1966.

Popper Karl, *The Logic of Scientific Discovery*, Hutchinson, 1959, 10th edn, 1980.

Popper, Karl, *Conjectures and Refutation: The Growth of Scientific Knowledge*, Routledge and Kegan Paul, 1963, rev. edn, 1972.

Popper, Karl, *Objective Knowledge: An Evolutionary Approach*, Clarendon Press, Oxford, 1972, rev. edn, 1979.

Popper, Karl, *Unended Quest: An Intellectual Autobiography*, Fontana 1976, rev. edn, 1986.

Prescott, W. H., *The Conquest of Peru*, 1847.

Prime, Ranchor, *The Illustrated Bhagavad Gita*, Godsfield Press, Alresford, 2002.

Qur'an, *The Holy Qur'an*, trans. Abdullah Yusuf Ali, Wordsworth Editions Ltd., 2000.

Ratzinger, Joseph (now Pope Benedict XVI), *In the Beginning: A Catholic Understanding of the Story of Creation and the Fall*, trans. Boniface Ramsey OP, T. and T. Clark, Edinburgh, 1995.

Rawls, John, *A Theory of Justice*, Oxford University Press, rev. edn, 2006.

Rees, Martin, *Before the Beginning: Our Universe and Others*, Simon and Schuster, 1997.

Rees, Martin, *Our Cosmic Habitat*, Weidenfeld and Nicolson, 2001.

Robinson, James R., *The Nag Hammadi Library in English,* HarperSanFrancisco, 1988.

Sagan, Karl, *Cosmos*, Random House, 1980.

Sanders, E. P., *Judaism: Practice and Belief 63 BCE – 66 CE*, SCM Press, 1992.

Sayer, George, *Jack: A Life of C. S. Lewis*, Hodder and Stoughton, 1988.

Schepps, Solomon J. (ed. and intro.), *The Lost Books of the Bible*, Testament Books, New York, 1979.

Simon, Bernard, *The Essence of the Gnostics*, Eagle Editions, Royston, 2004.

Smalley, Beryl, *The Study of the Bible in the Middle Ages,* Clarendon Press, 1941.

Socrates, *The Ecclesiastical History of Socrates, surnamed Scholasticus or the Advocate*, Bohn's Ecclesiastical Library, 1853.

Sozomen, *The Ecclesiastical History of Sozomen*, Bohn's Ecclesiastical Library, 1855.

Sparks, H. F. D., 'Jerome as Biblical Scholar', *Cambridge History of the Bible*, vol. 1, Cambridge University Press, 1975.

Stachel, John (ed.), *Einstein's Marvellous Year: Five Papers that Changed the Face of Physics*, Princeton University Press, 1998.

Stewart, Ian, *Life's Other Secret*, Allen Lane, 1998.

Temple, William, *Readings in St John's Gospel*, Macmillan, 1939–40.

Thomas Aquinas, Complete Works in Latin, Parma edn, 25 vols, 1852–72, reprinted New York, 1948. English translations include *The Summa Theologica*, 22 vols, 1912–26, and *The Summa Contra Gentiles*, 5 vols, 1928–29.

Tongeren, Paul van, *et al.* (eds), *Searching for Peace in Europe and Eurasia: An Overview of Conflict Prevention and Peacebuilding Activities*, European Centre for Conflict Prevention, Utrecht, 2002.

Tongeren, Paul van, *et al.* (eds.), *People Building Peace II: Successful Stories of Civil Society*, European Centre for Conflict Prevention, Utrecht, 2005.

Vatican Observatory, *Physics, Philosophy and Theology*, Vatican State, 1988,

Watson, James D., *The Double Helix: A Personal Account of the Discovery of the Structure of DNA*, Penguin, 1999.

Weber, Max, *On Charisma and Institution Building* (ed. and intro. S. N. Eisenstadt), University of Chicago Press, 1968.

Wessels, Anton, *Understanding the Qur'an*, SCM Press, 2000.

Williams, A. L., (trans. and ed.), *Justin Martyr, The Dialogue with Trypho*, New York, 1930.

Williams, Rowan, *Writing in the Dust: Reflections on 11th September and Its Aftermath*, Hodder and Stoughton, 2002.

Williams, Rowan, *Christ on Trial*, Zondervan, Grand Rapids, 2002.

Williams, Rowan, *Open to Judgement,* Darton, Longman and Todd, 2002.

Wilmut, Ian, and Highfield, Roger, *After Dolly: The Uses and Misuses of Human Cloning*, Little Brown, 2006.

Wolde, Ellen van, *Stories of the Beginning: Genesis 1 – 11 and other Creation Stories*, trans. John Bowden, SCM Press, 1996.

Wolfson, Adrian, *Life Without Genes: The History and Future of Genomes*, Flamingo, 2000.

Wright, Tom, *Judas and the Gospel of Jesus*, SPCK, 2002.

Young, Frances, *The Making of the Creeds*, SCM Press, 1991.

Index

Tolkien, J. R. R., 164–5
Trinity, Holy, *see* Holy
Trinity
Triumphalism, 64–5, 70–1
True Cross, 105
Truth and Reconciliation
Committee, 157
Tsunami, 161
Tulip Revolution, 157
Tutu, Desmond, 144, 157
Twain, Mark, 171
Tyndale, William, 74

Uniqueness, human 35, 142,
see DNA
United Nations 141

Vatican Observatory, 31–2
Velvet Revolution, 157
Virgin Mary, 89, 90, 92–5,
96
Viruses, 16, 19
Vision, restricted, 2, 21, 41,

49, 92, 164, 166, 168,
188
Voodoo, 16
Vulgate, 74, 121, 126

Wallace, Alfred R., 10
Watson, James, 27–8
Weber, Max, 127
Wilberforce, Samuel, 11
Williams, Rowan, 137,
144–5, 162
Witches, 73, 135, 138
Wonder, sense of, 20, 133,
139, 164
Works of Mercy, 146
Worm-holes, 31

Zeitgeist, 141, 143
Zoe, 183, 185
Zoology, zoologists, 6–7,
125
see also Biologists,
Ethology